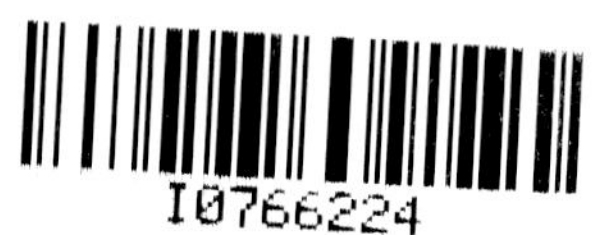

Cute Cat

Stress Relieving Designs for Adults Relaxation

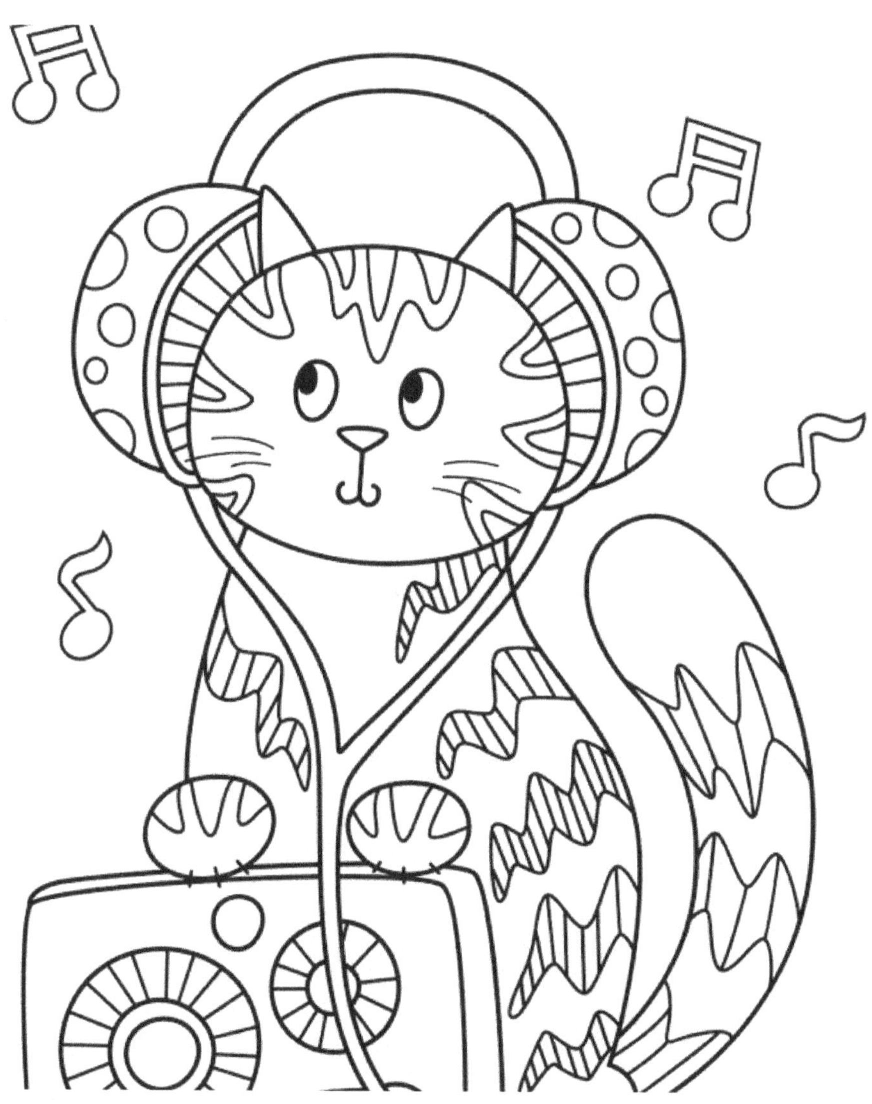

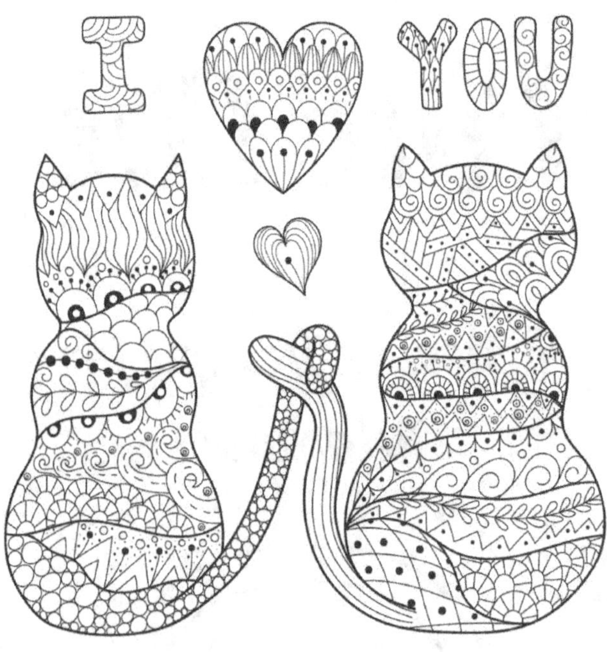

This ColoringBook Is Belongs To

____

____

____

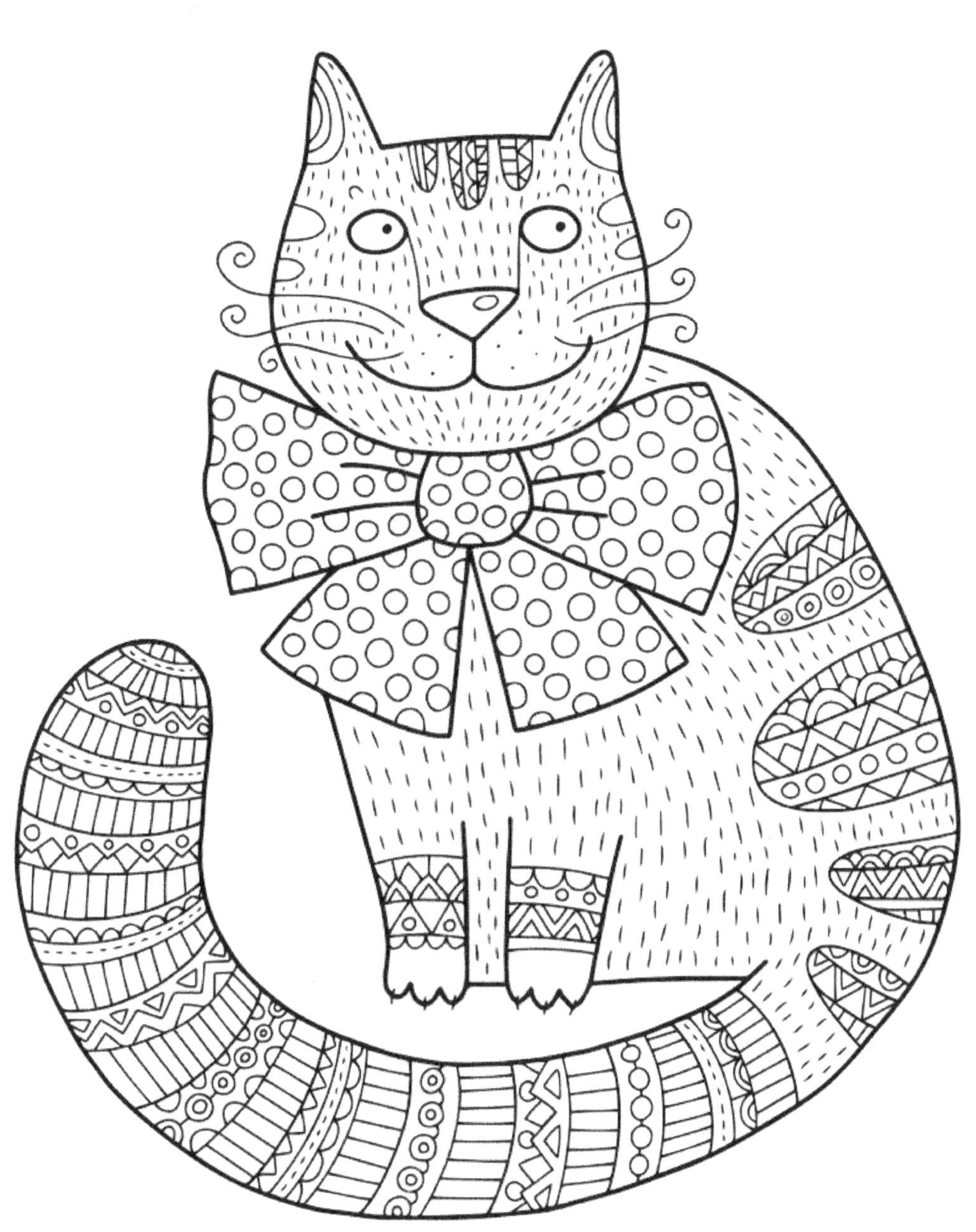

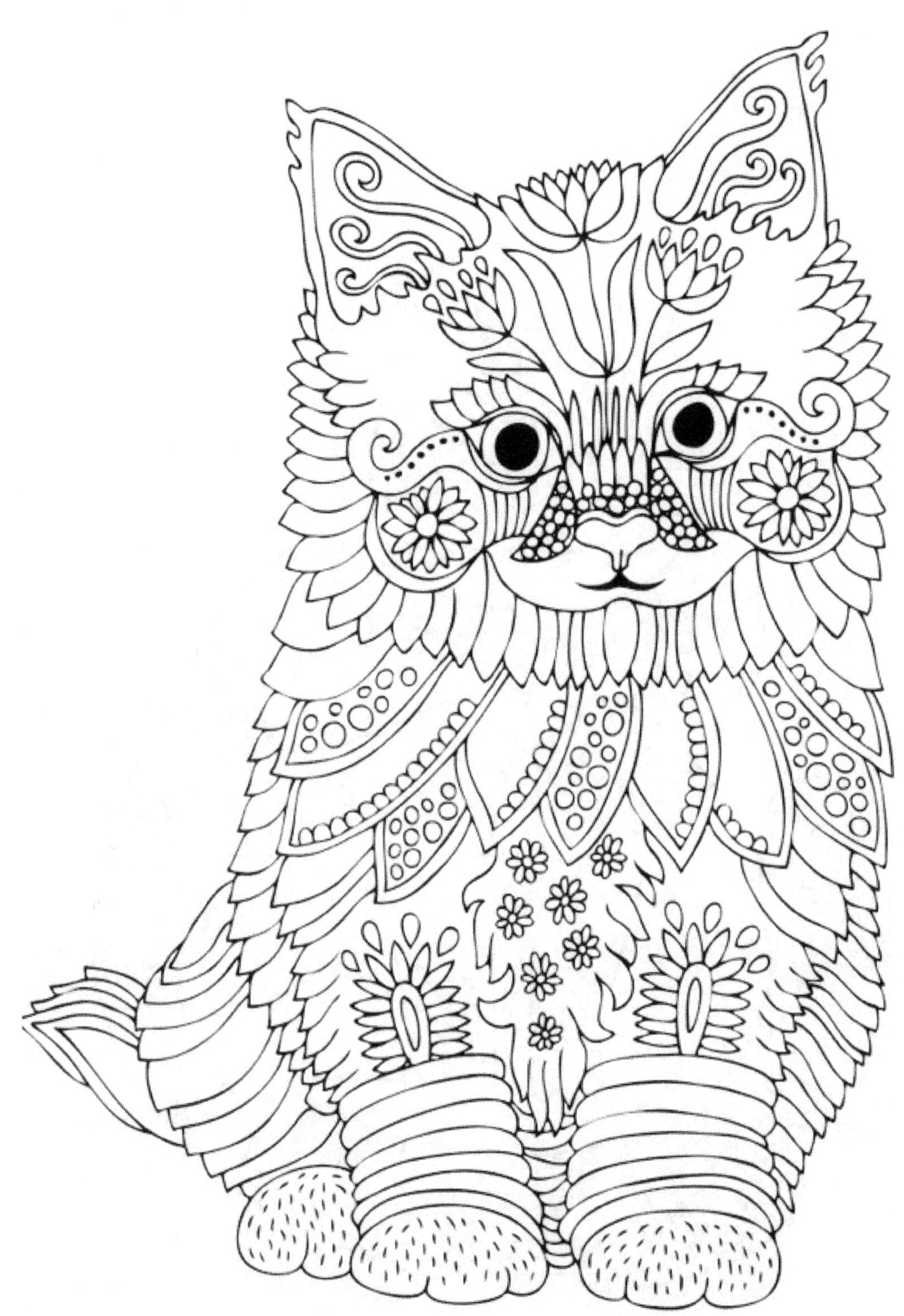

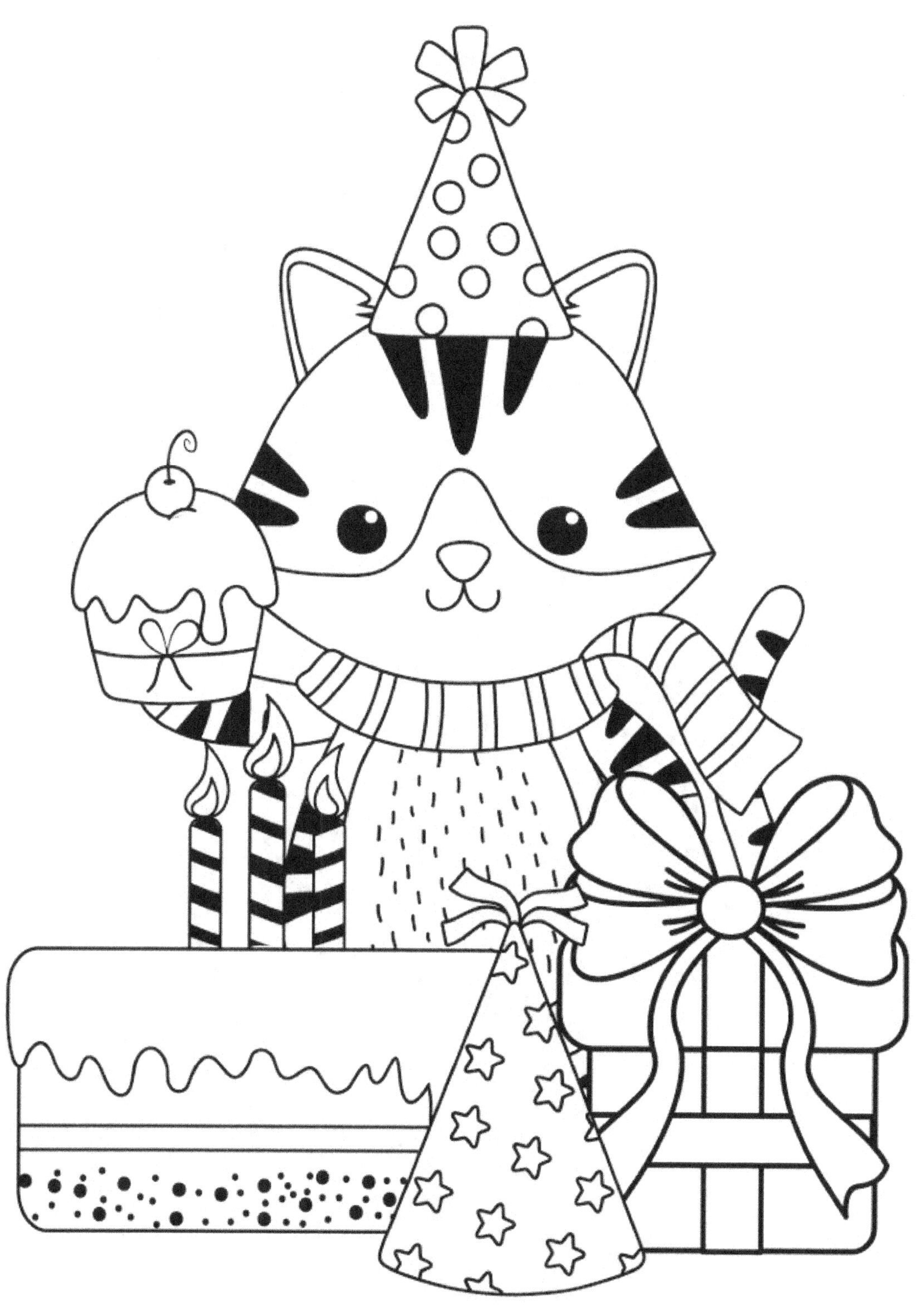

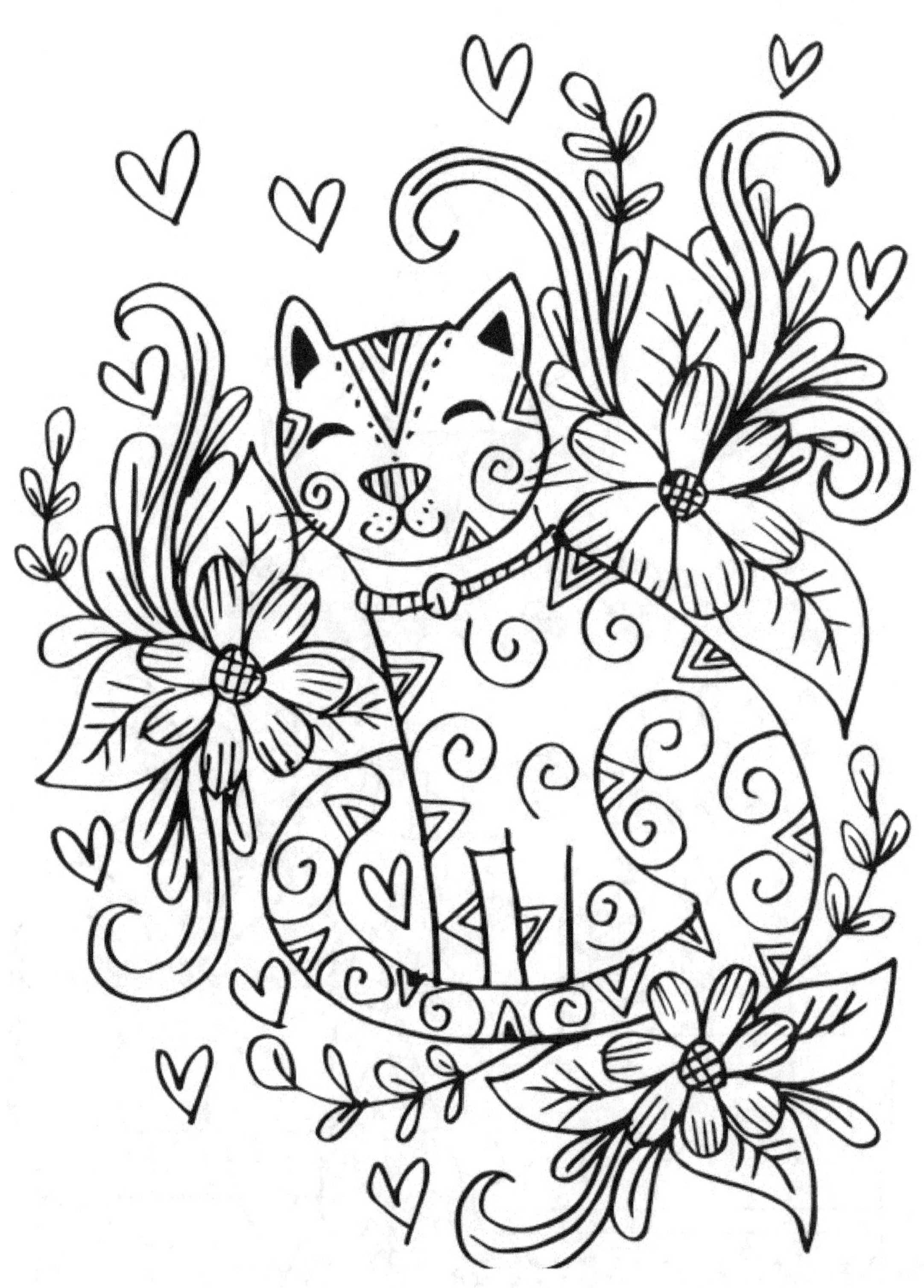

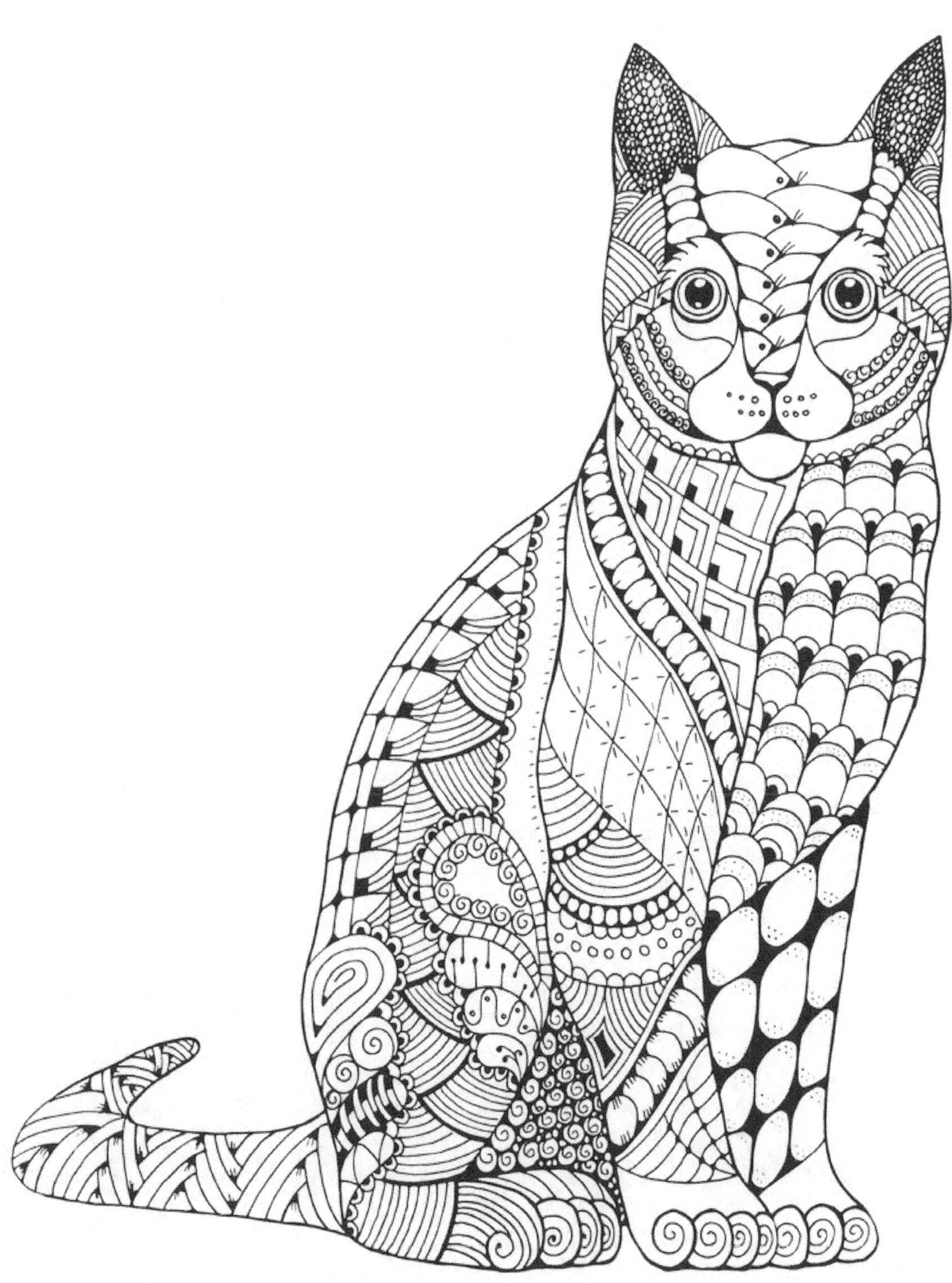

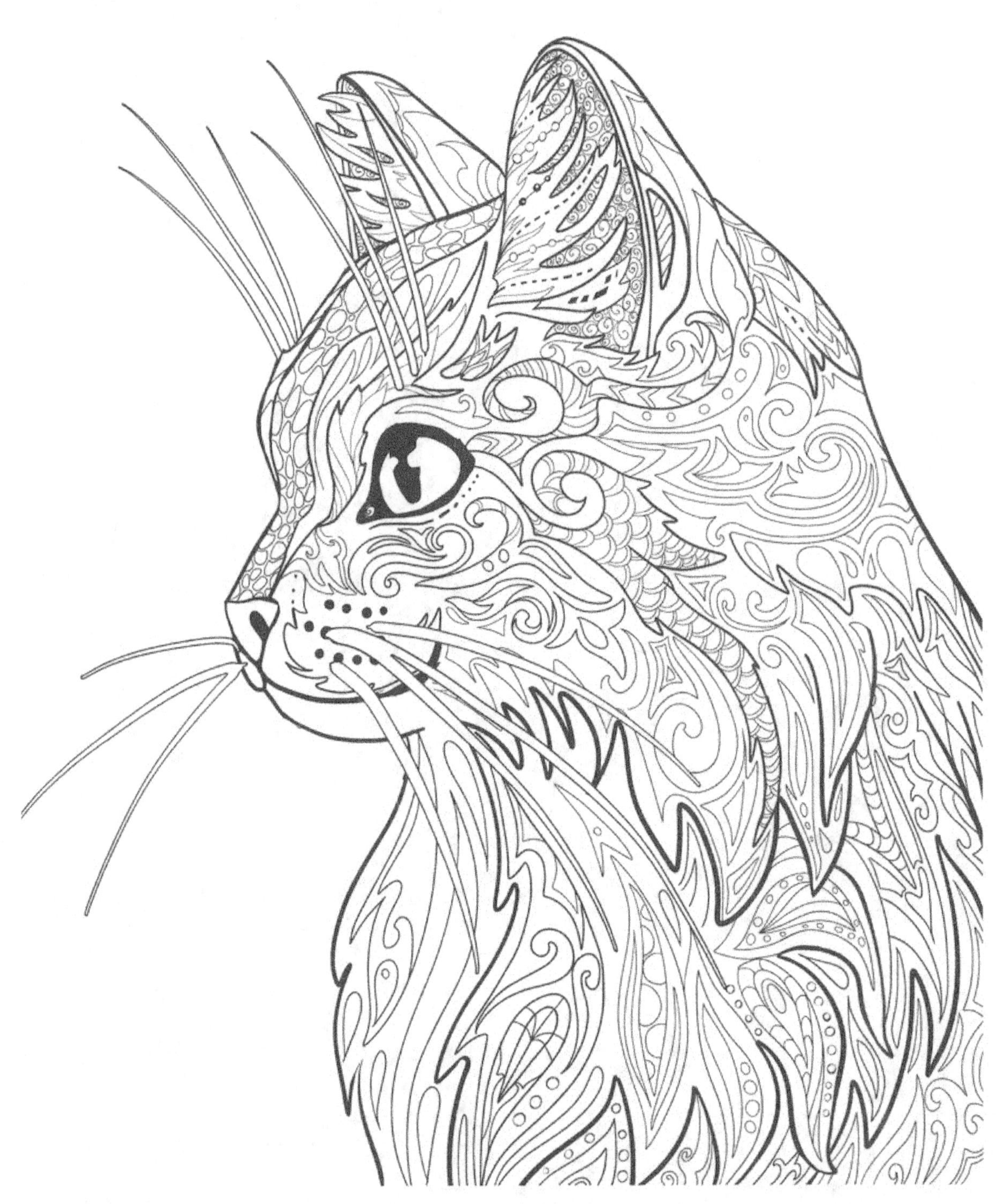

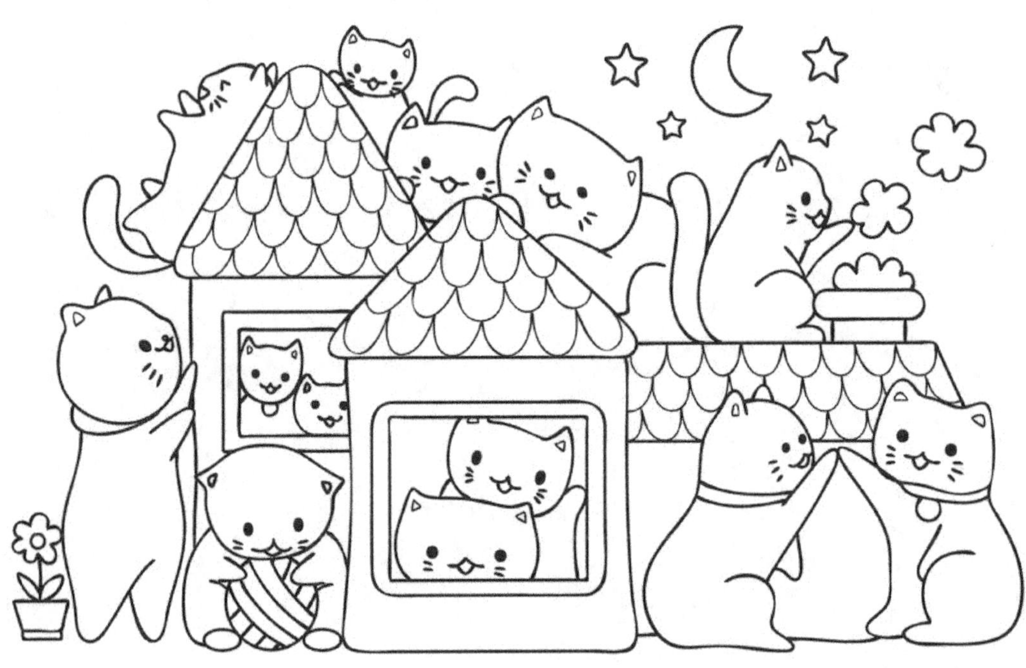

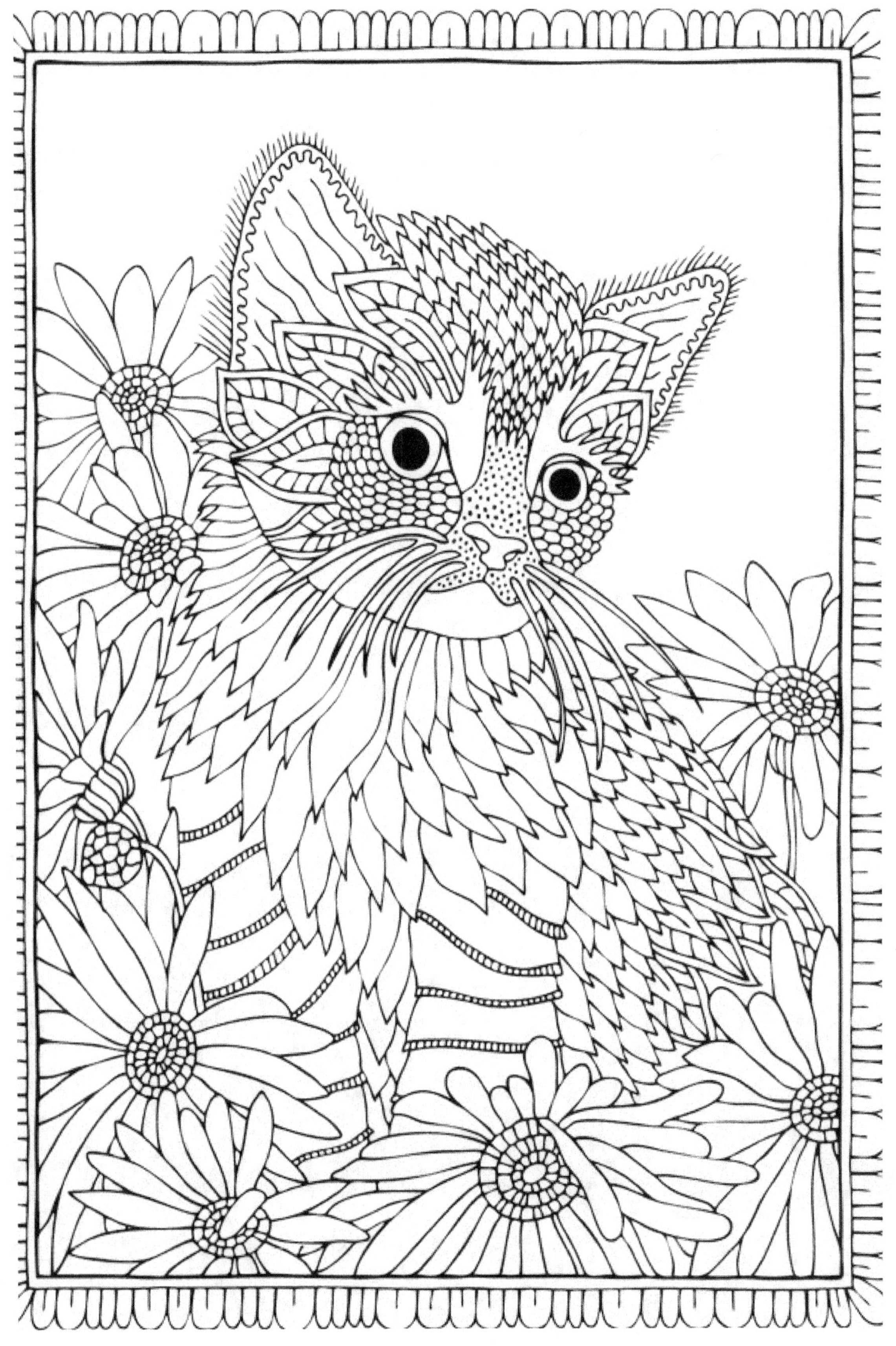

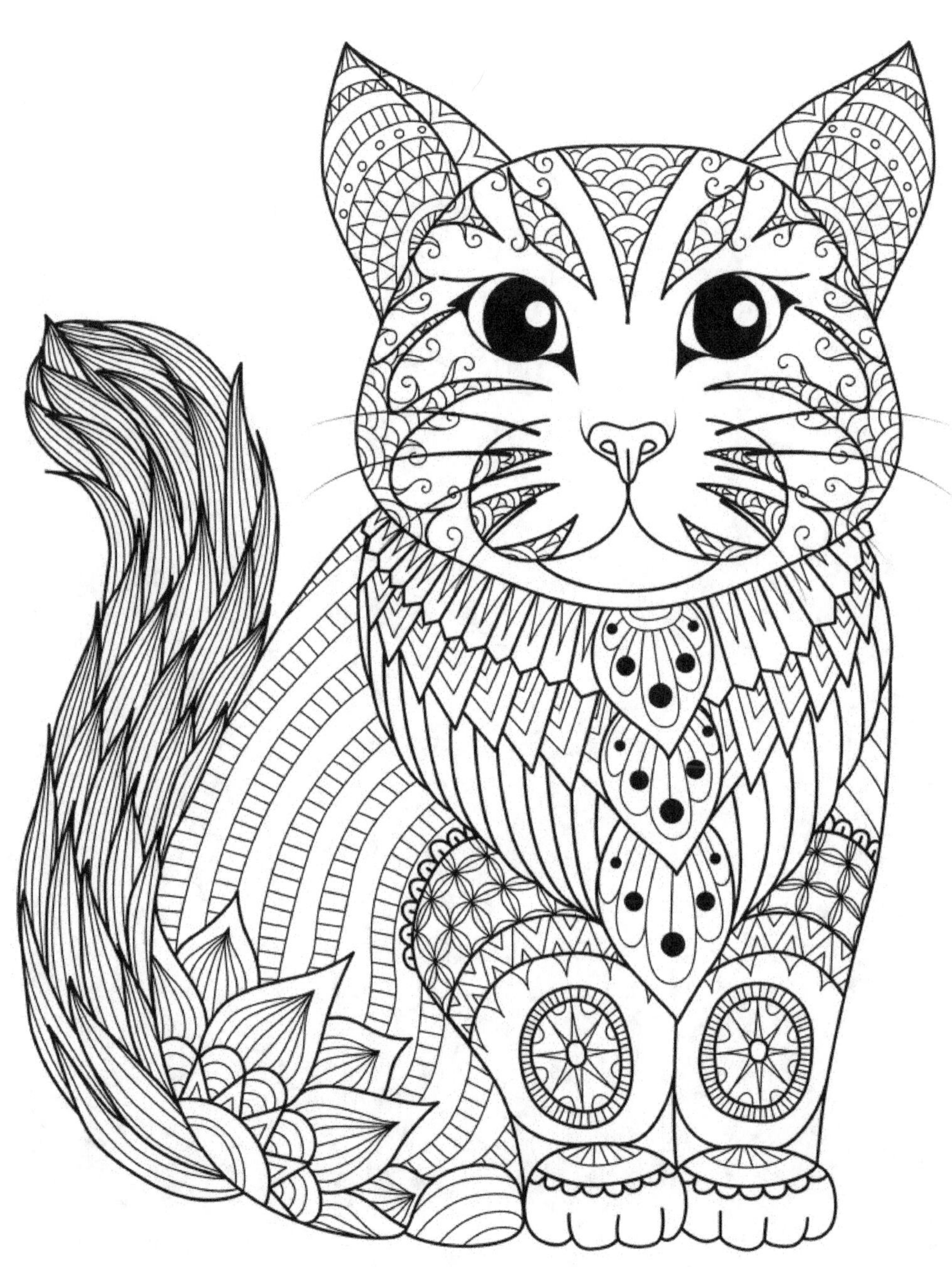

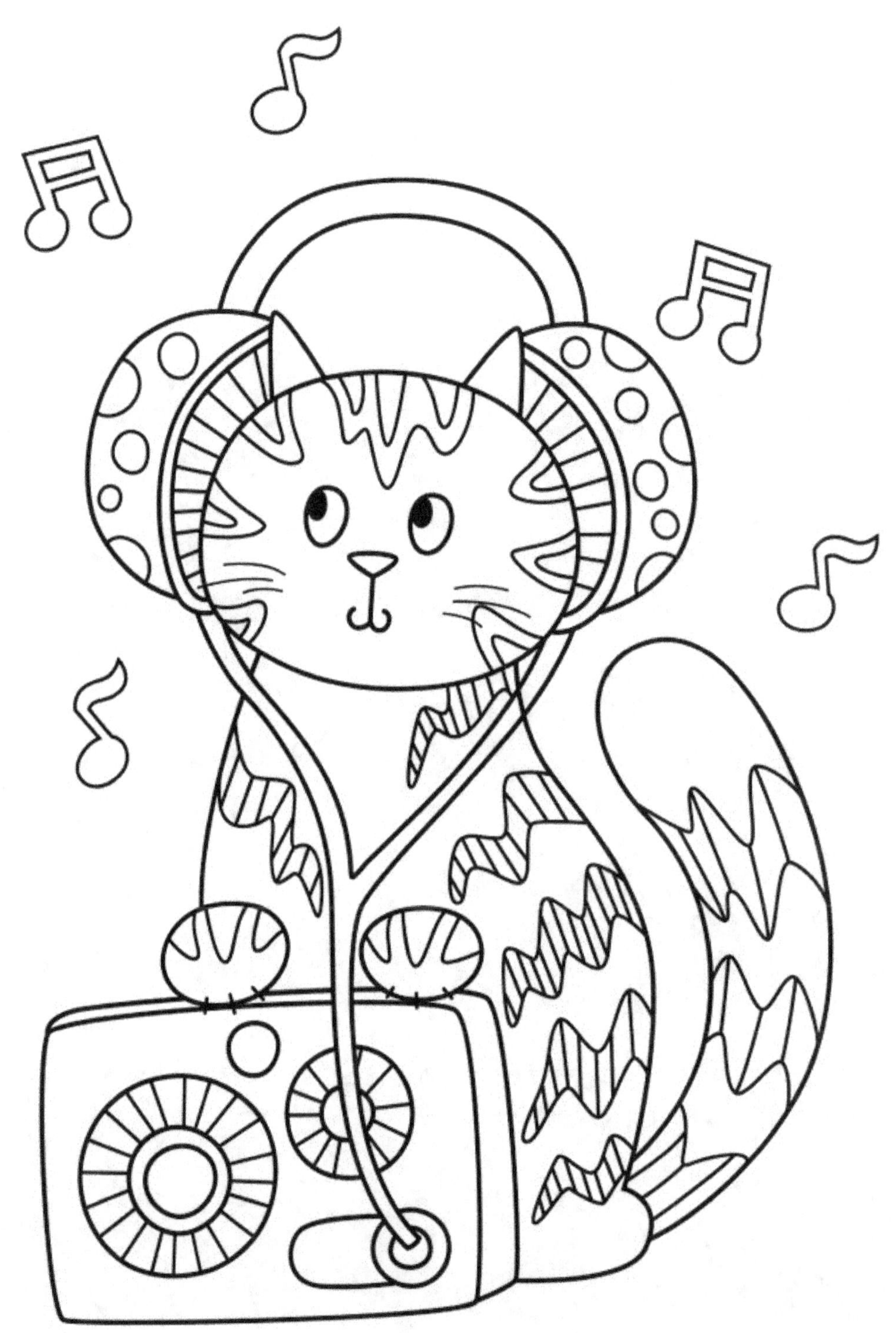

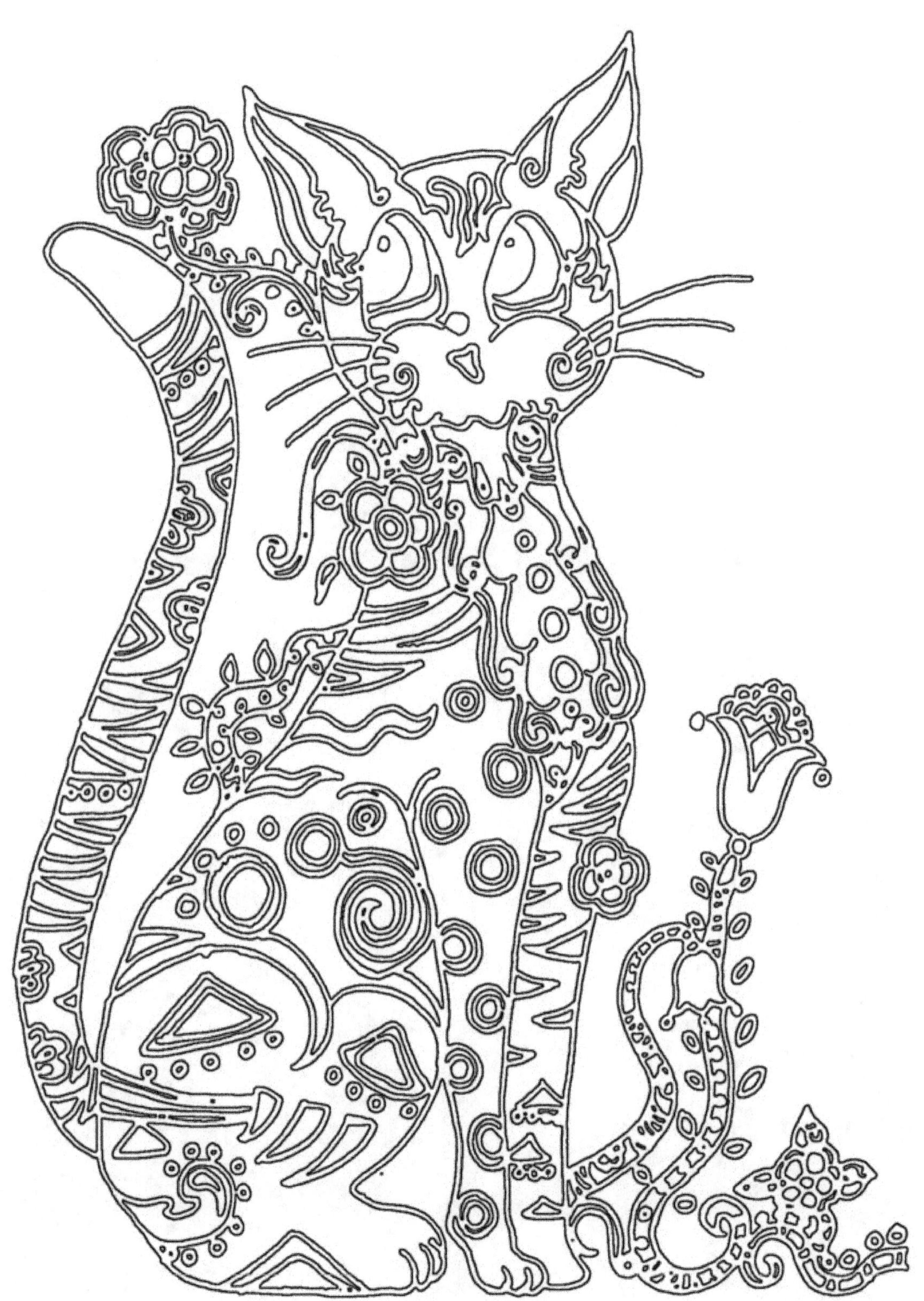

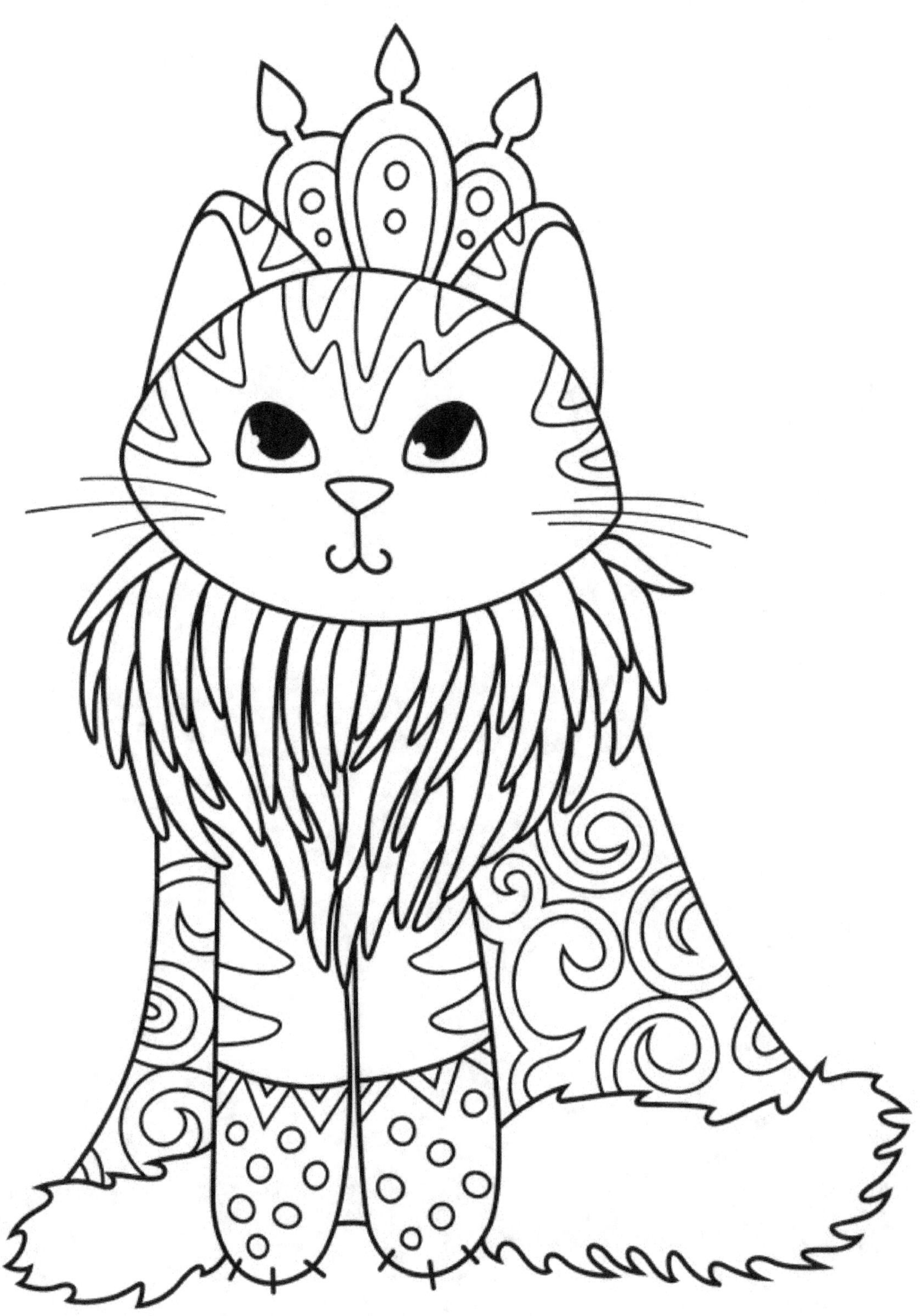

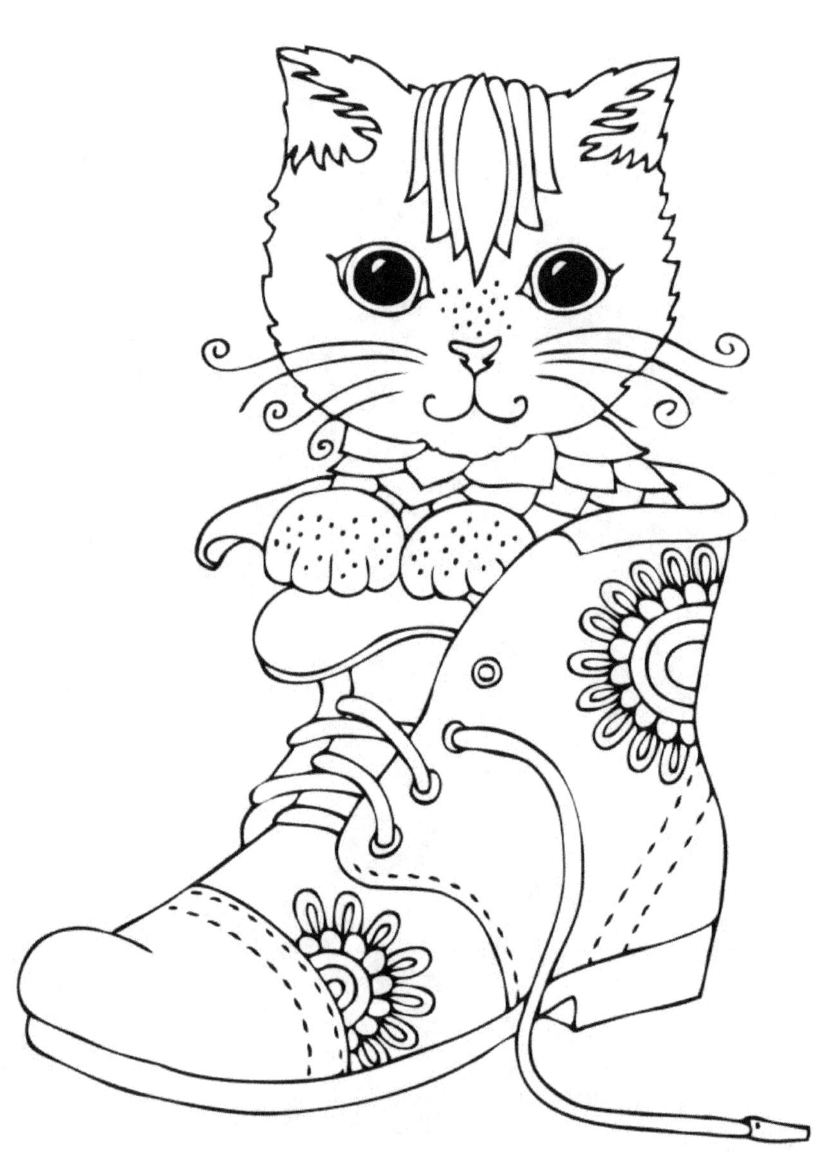

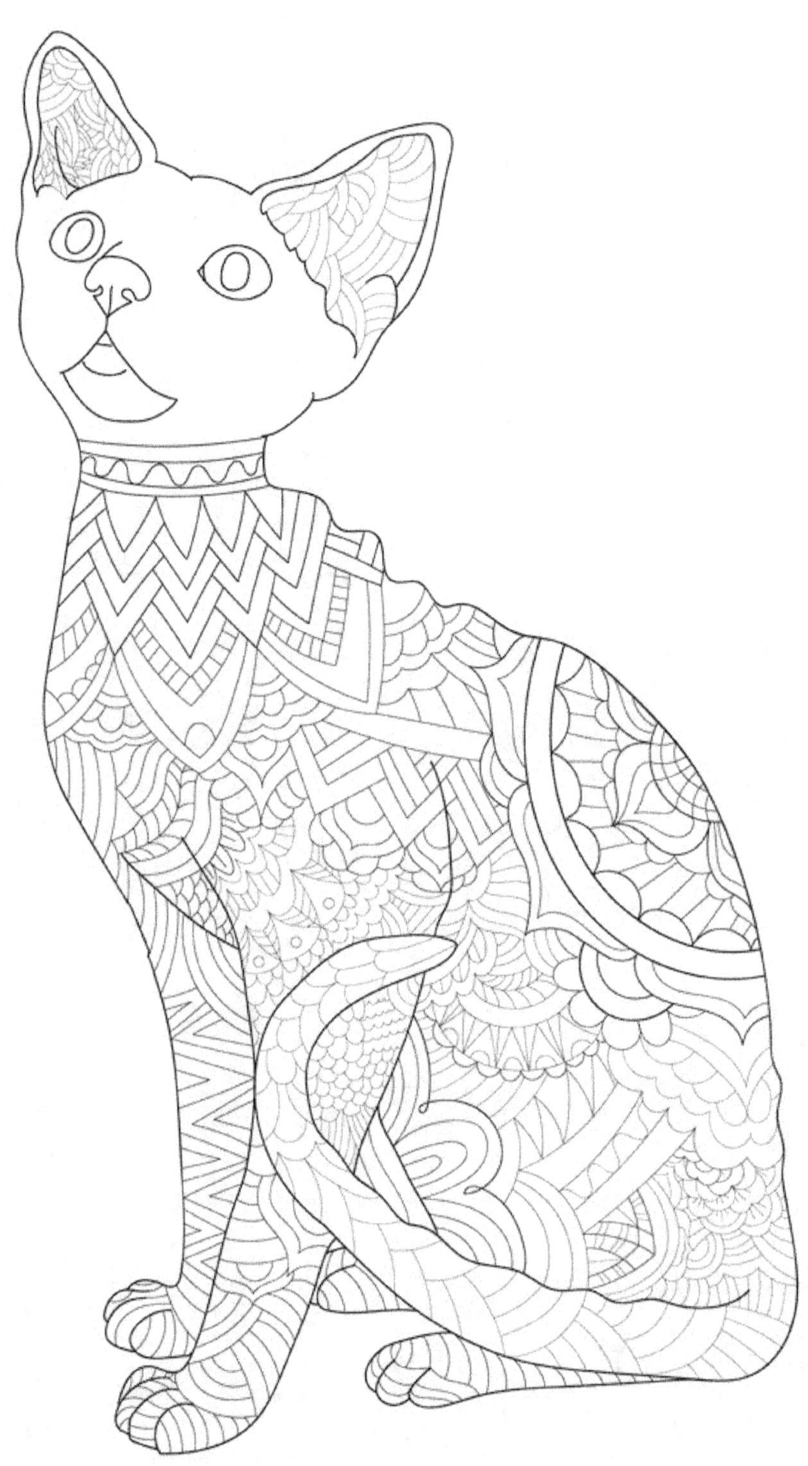

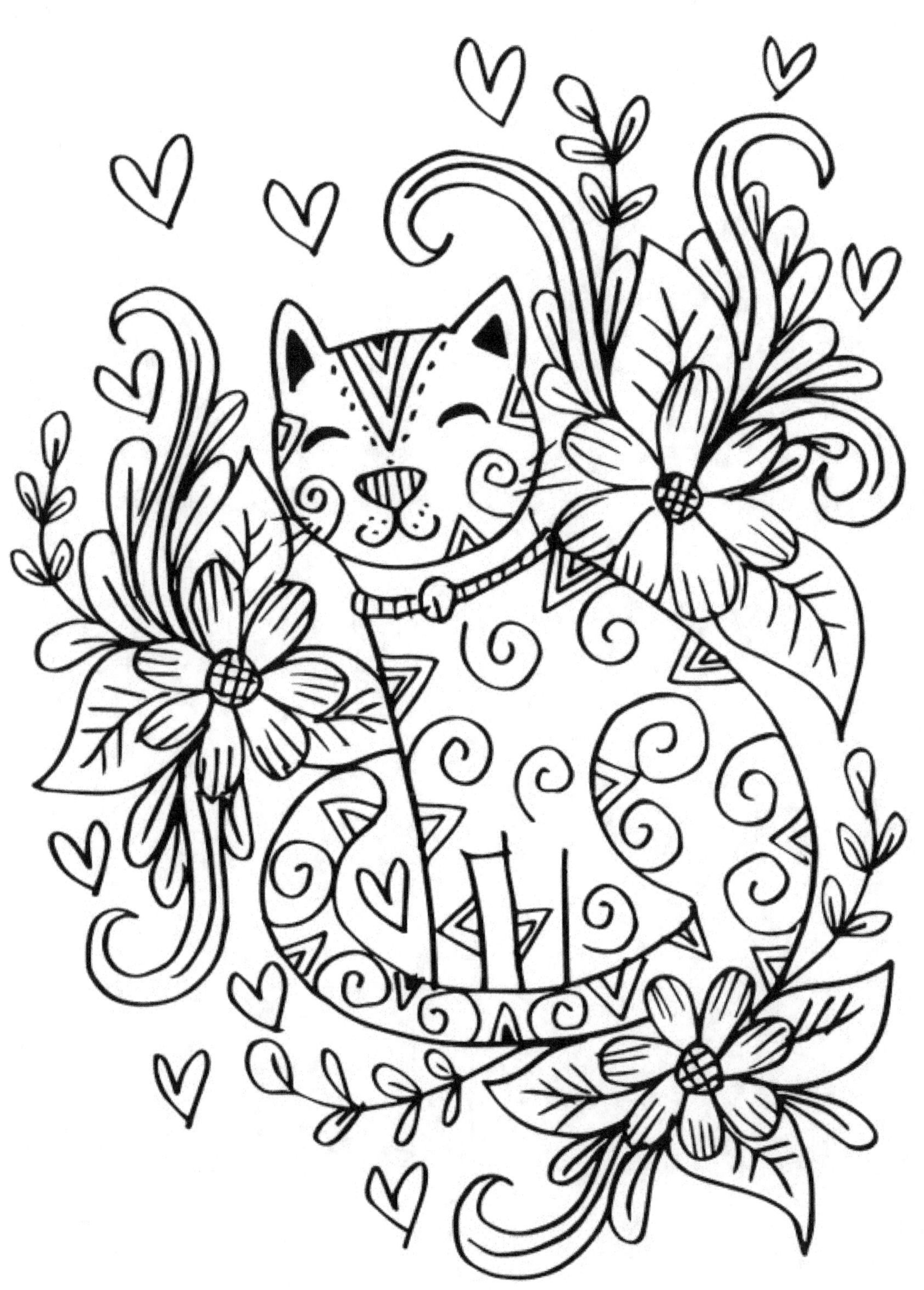

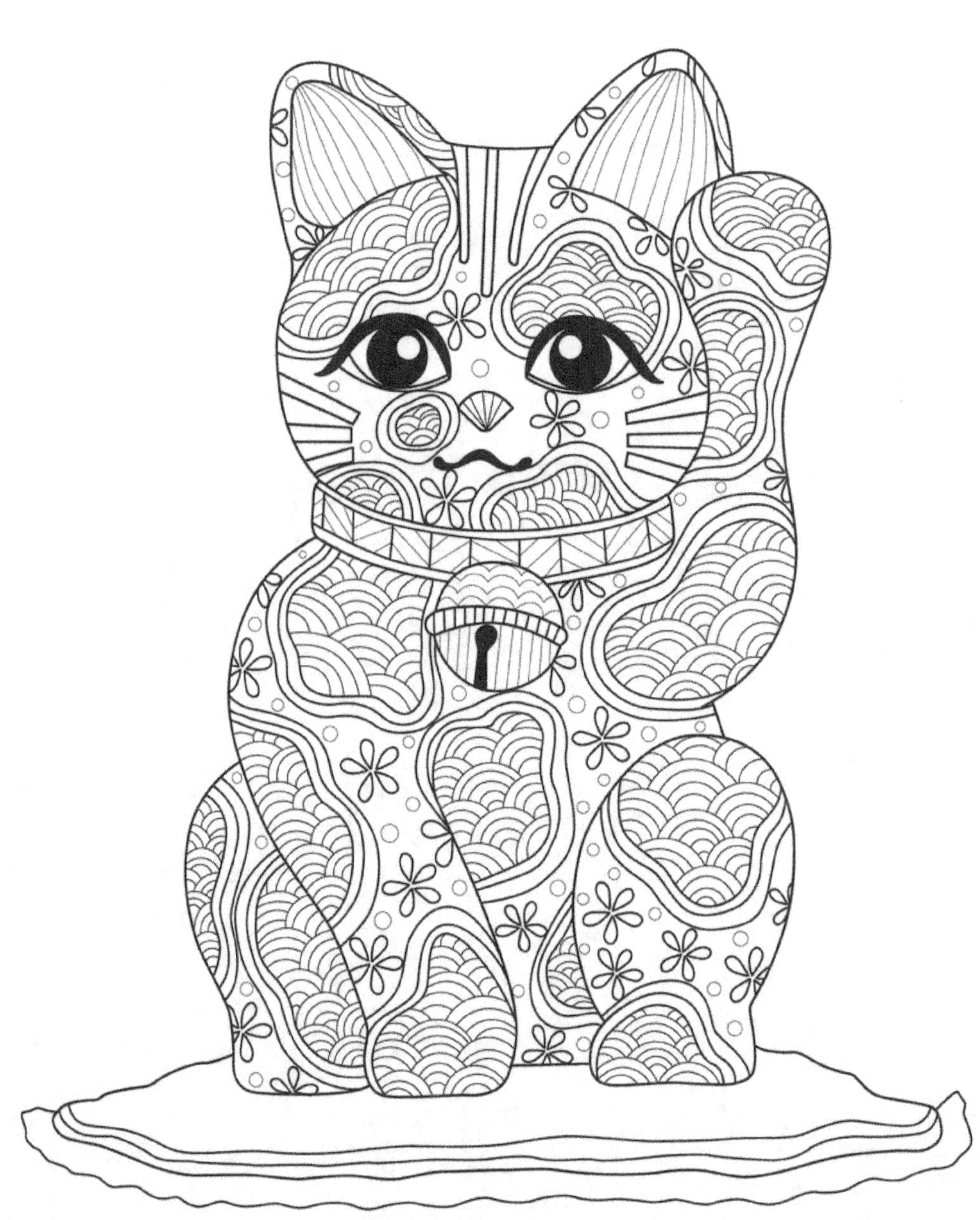

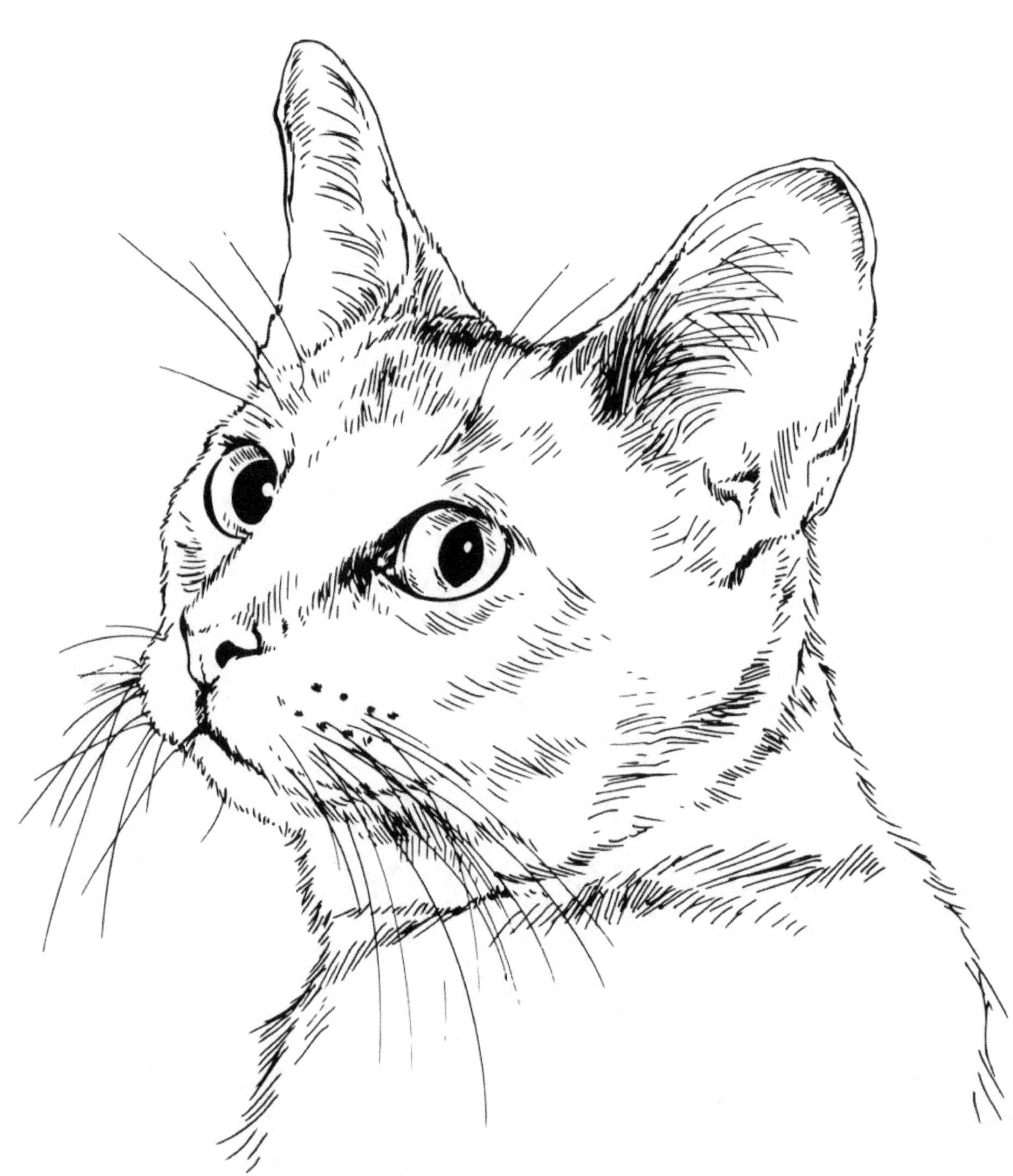

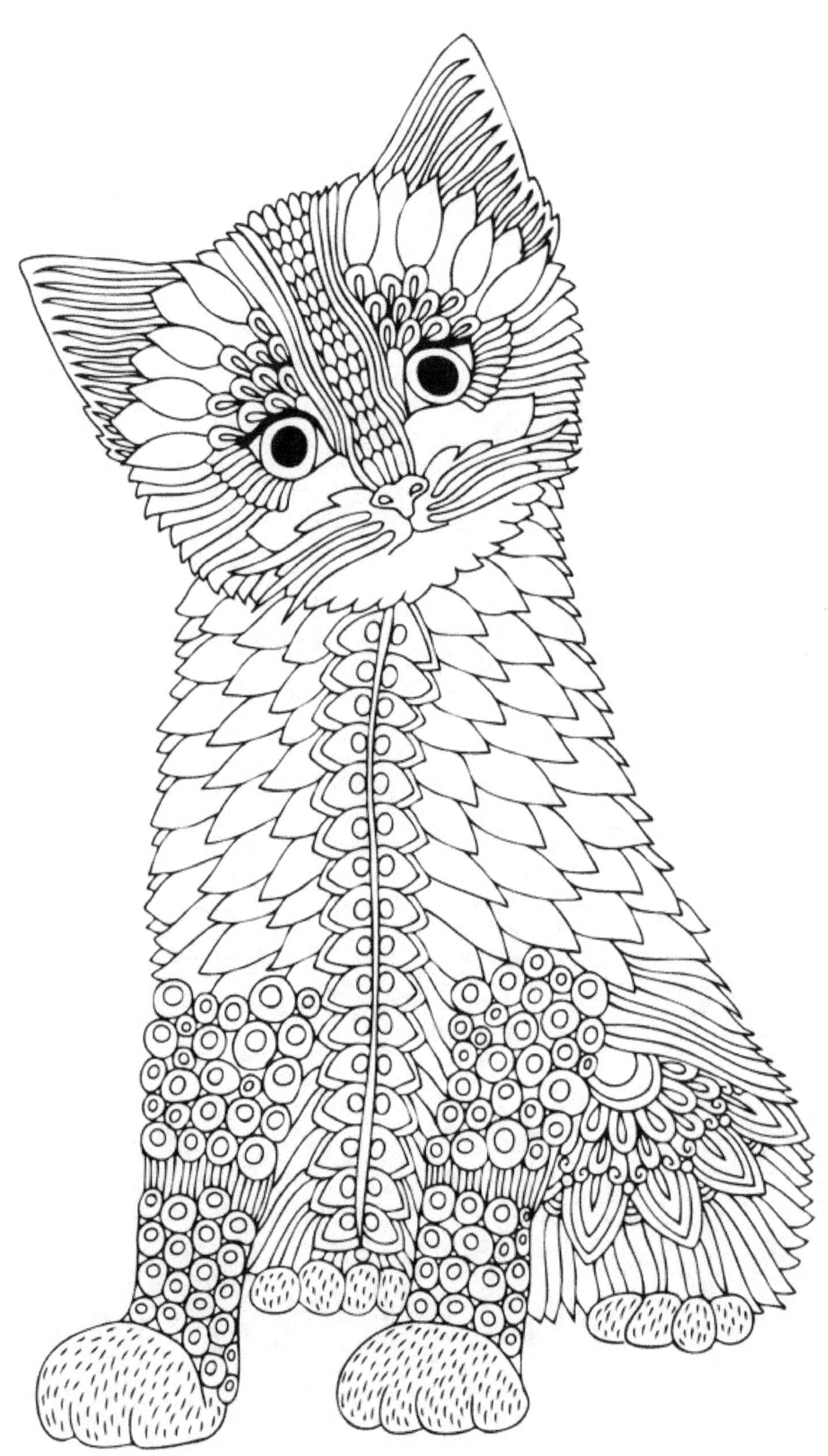

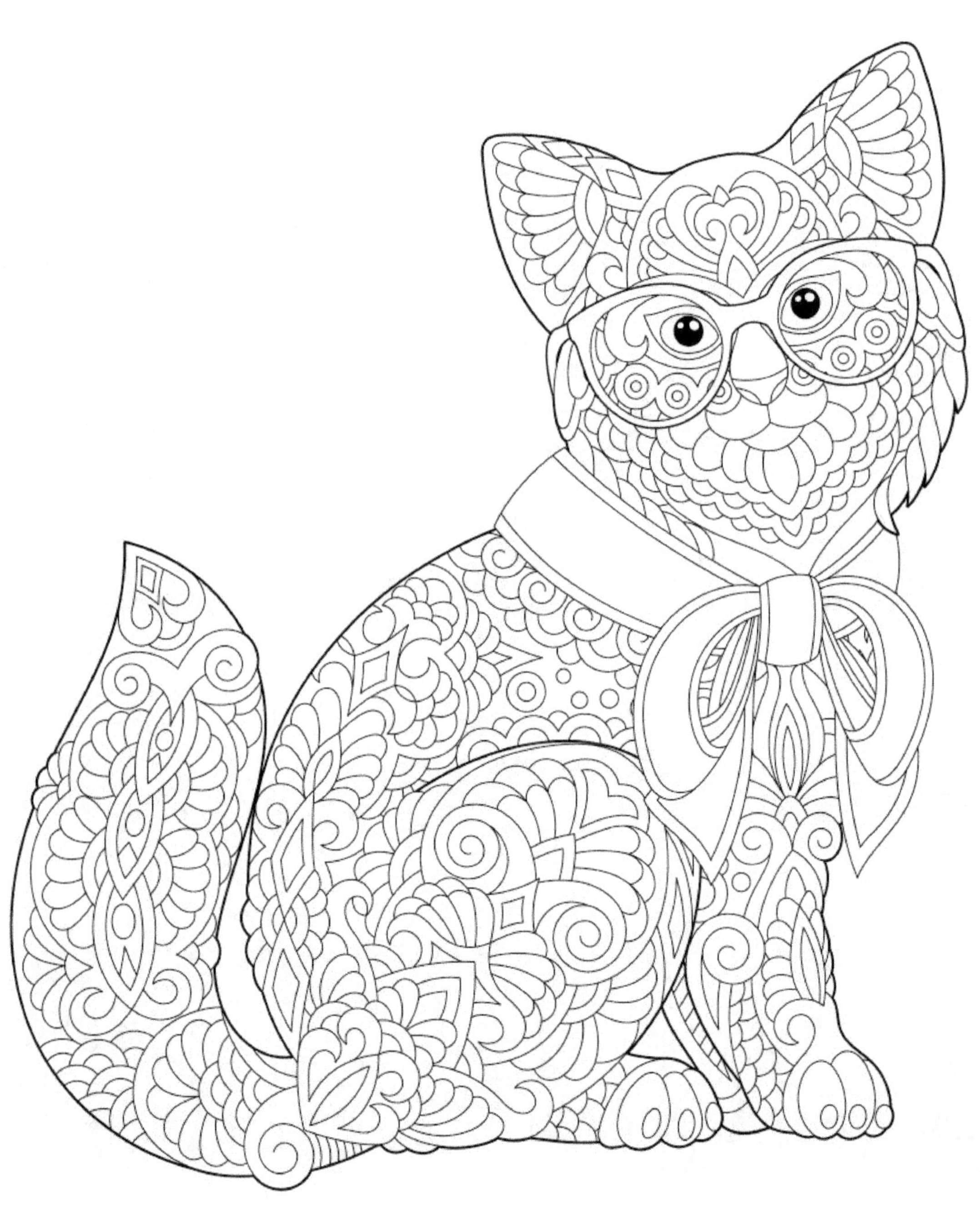

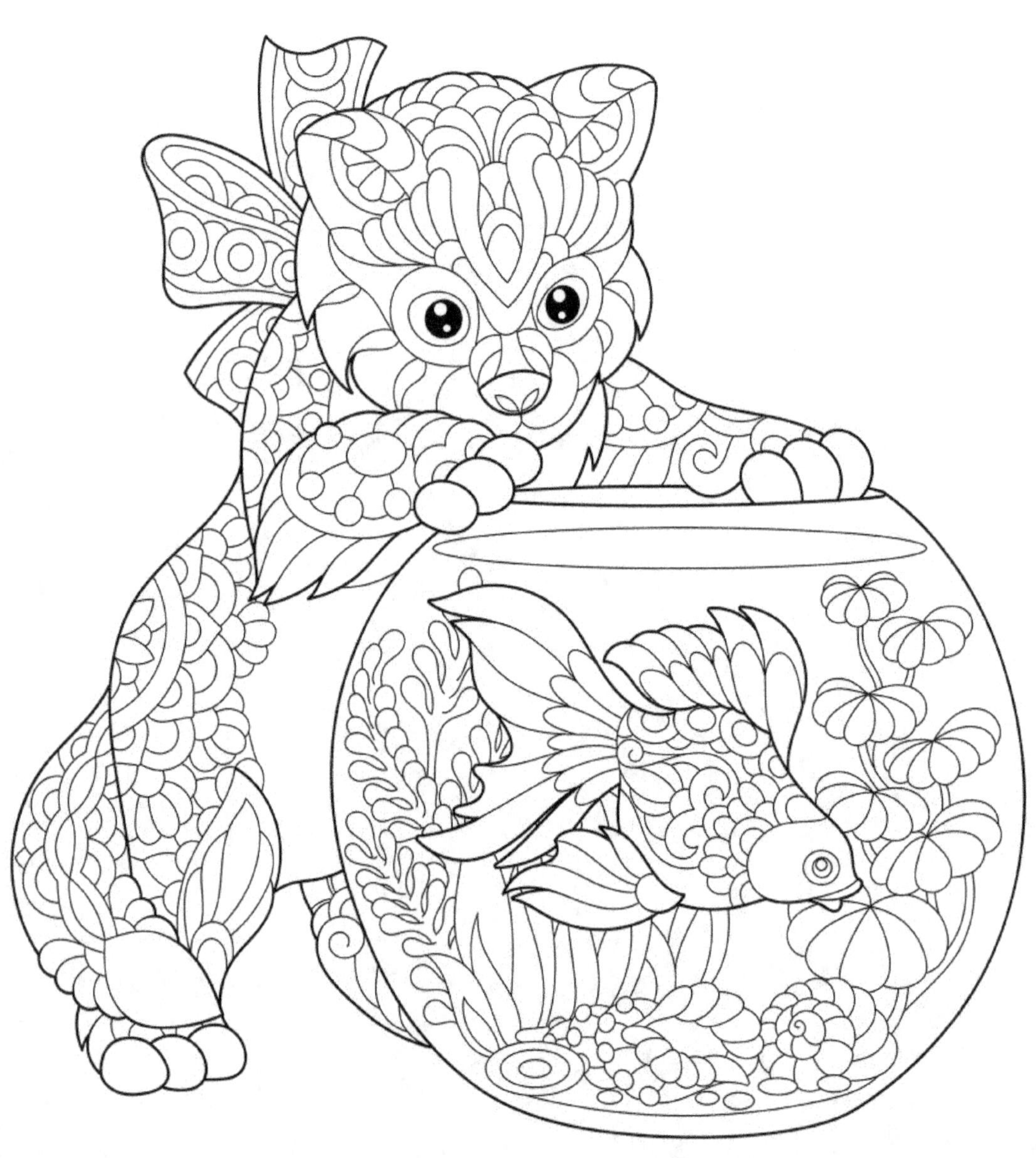

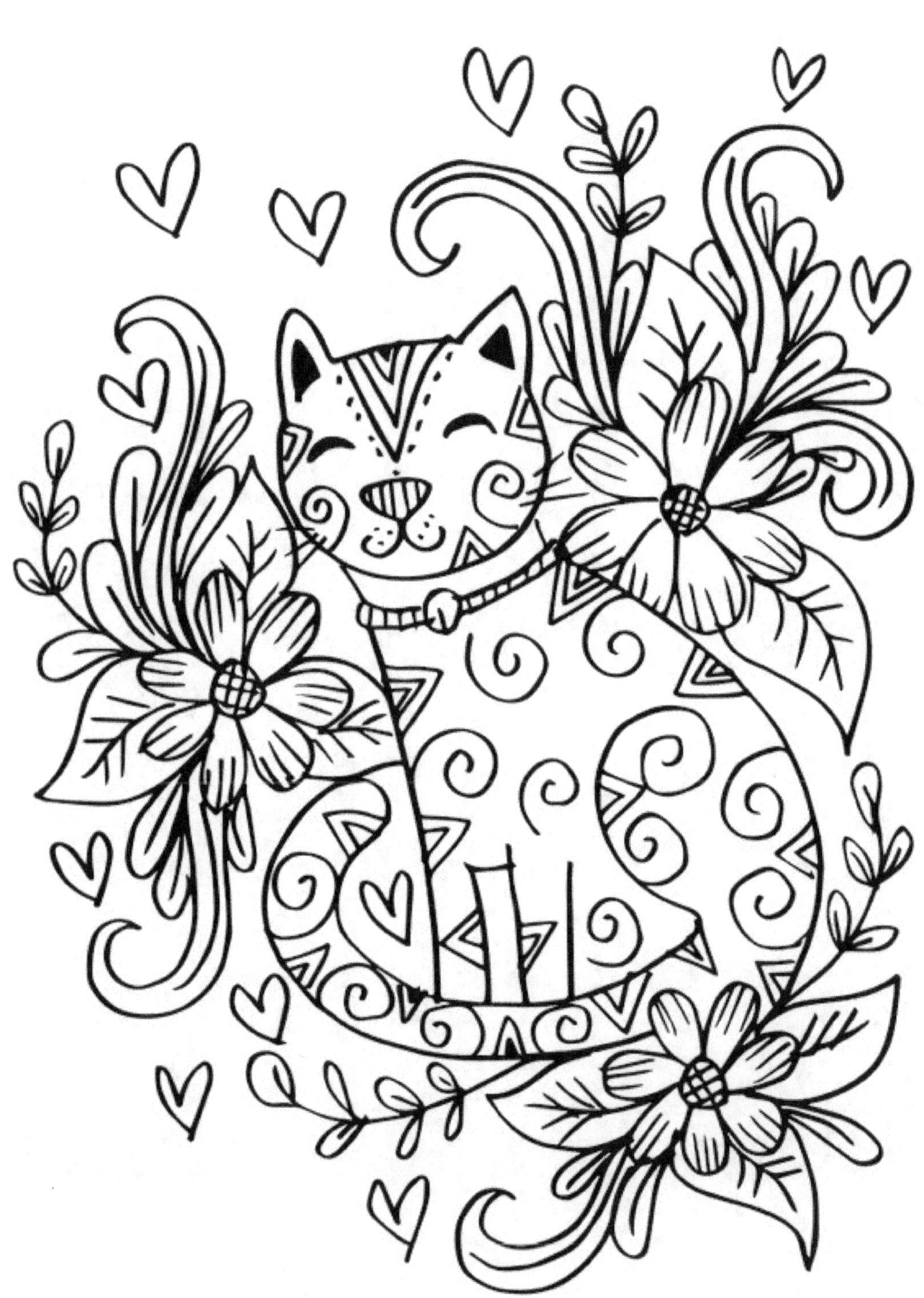

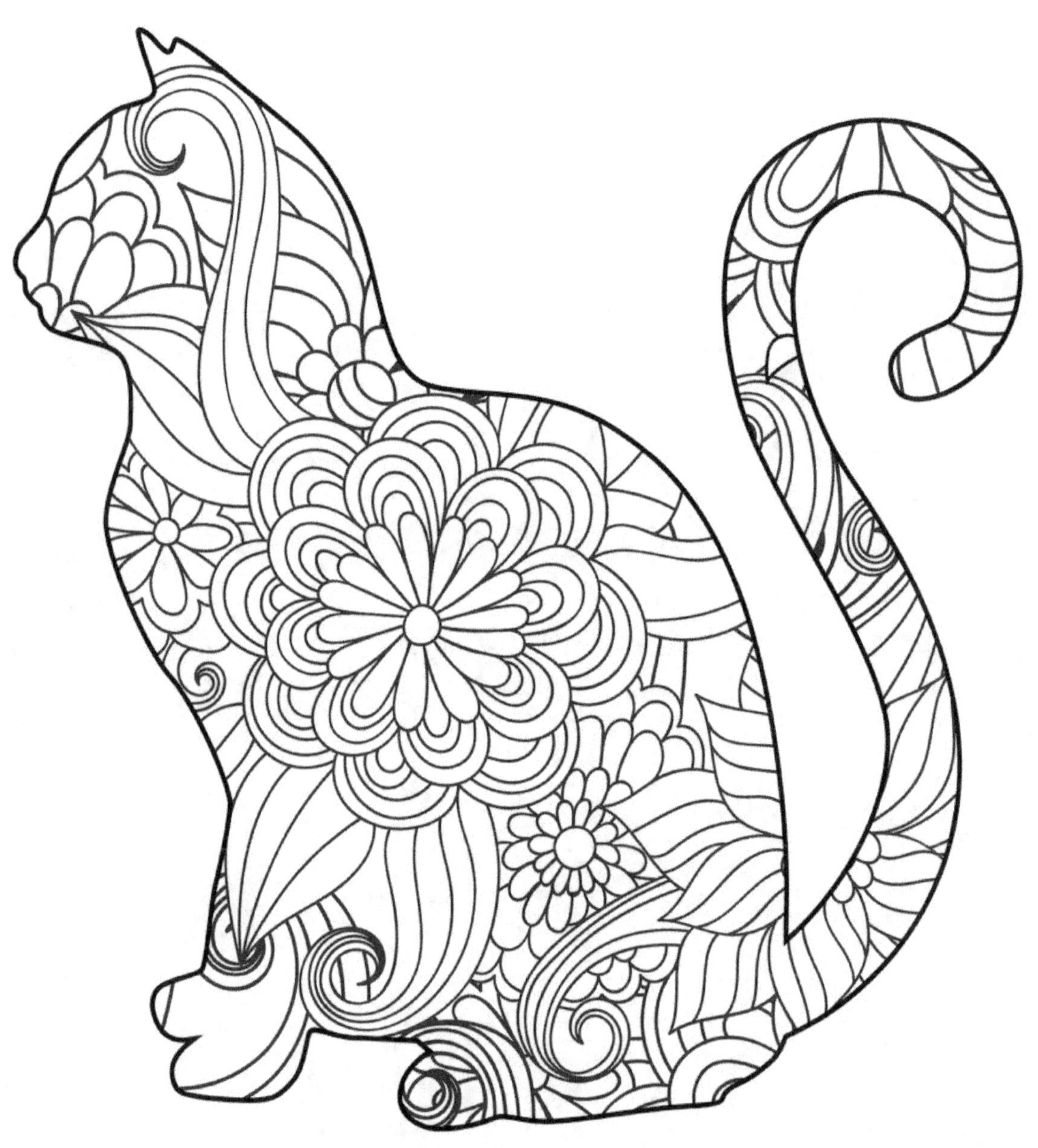

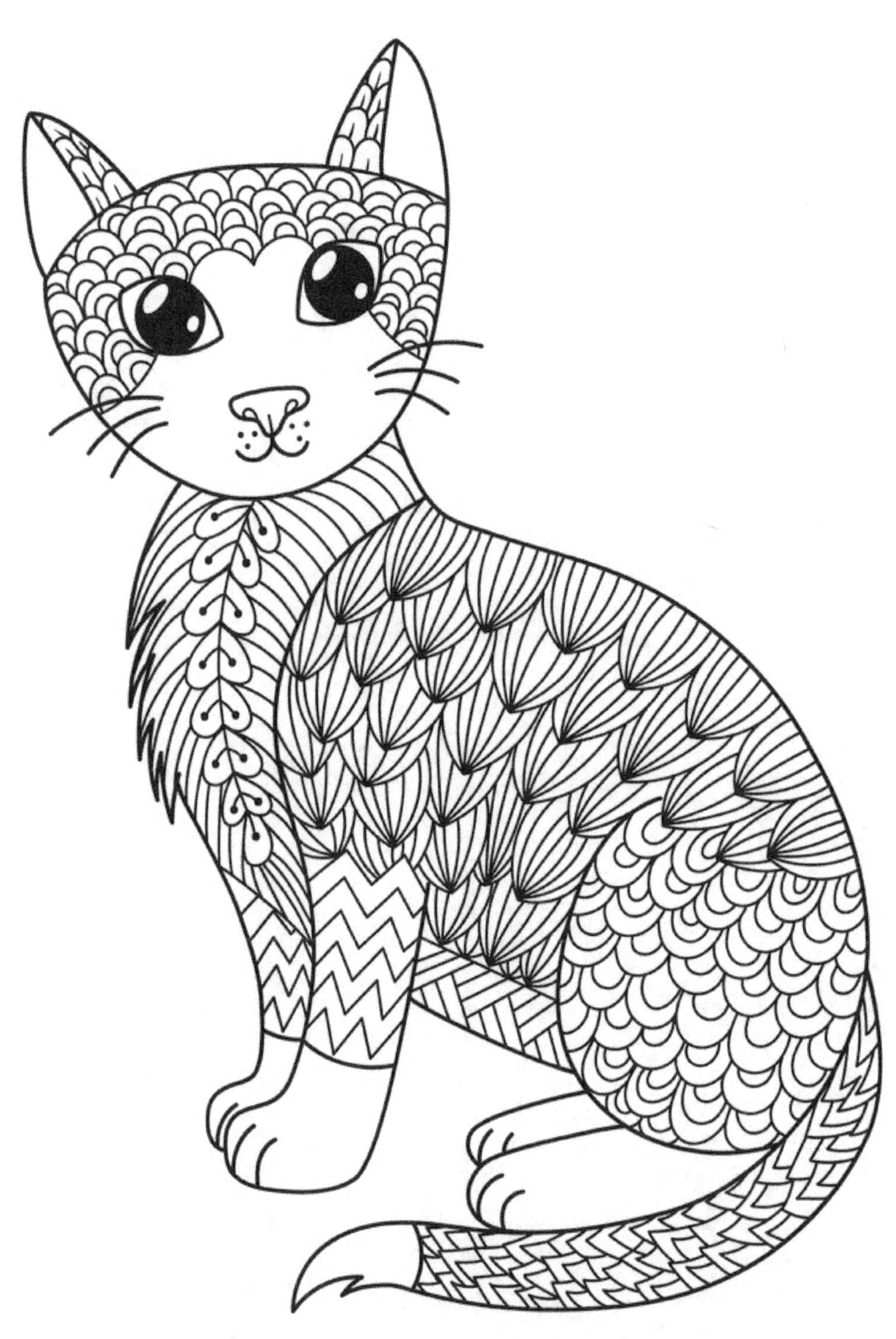

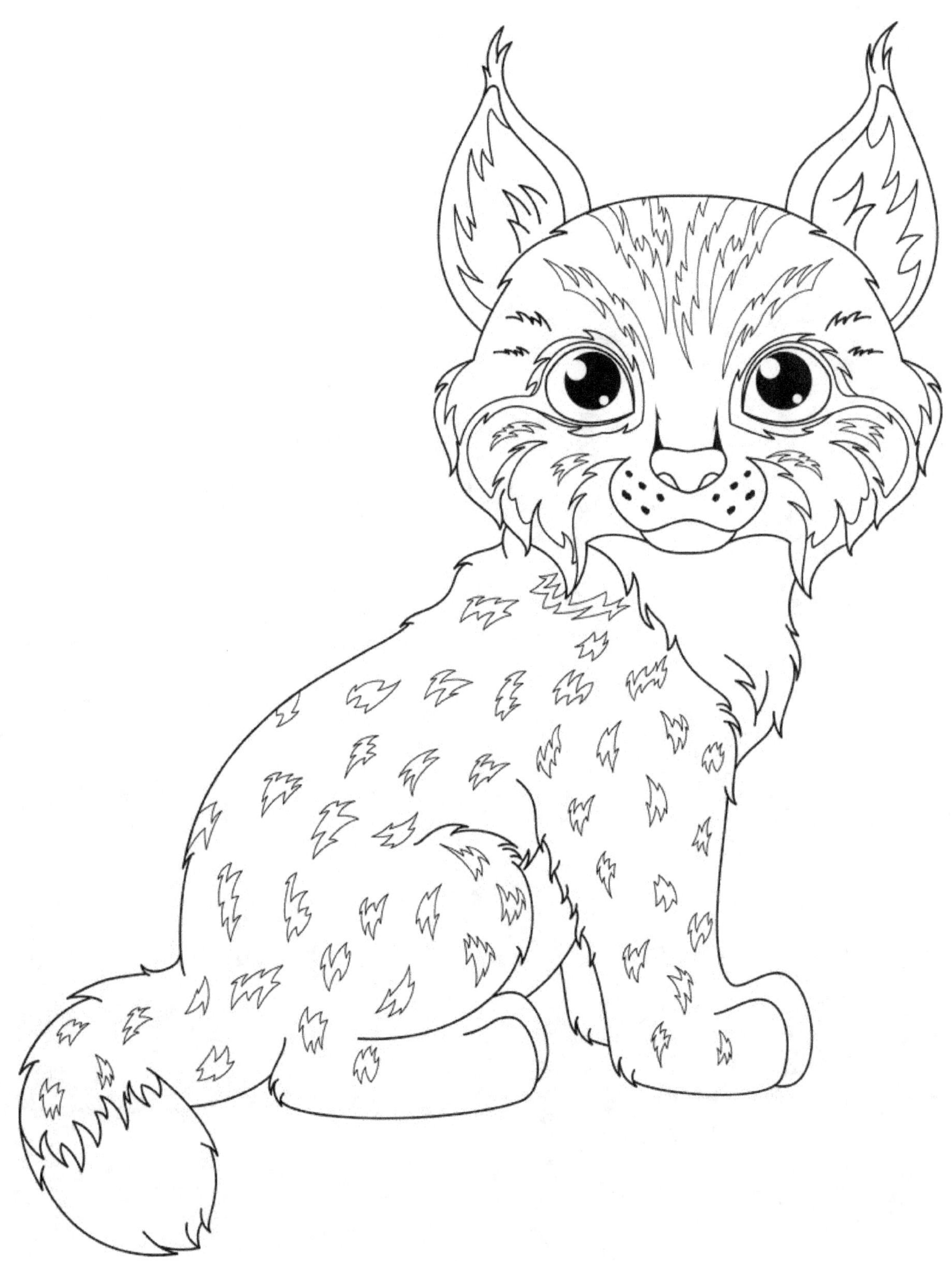

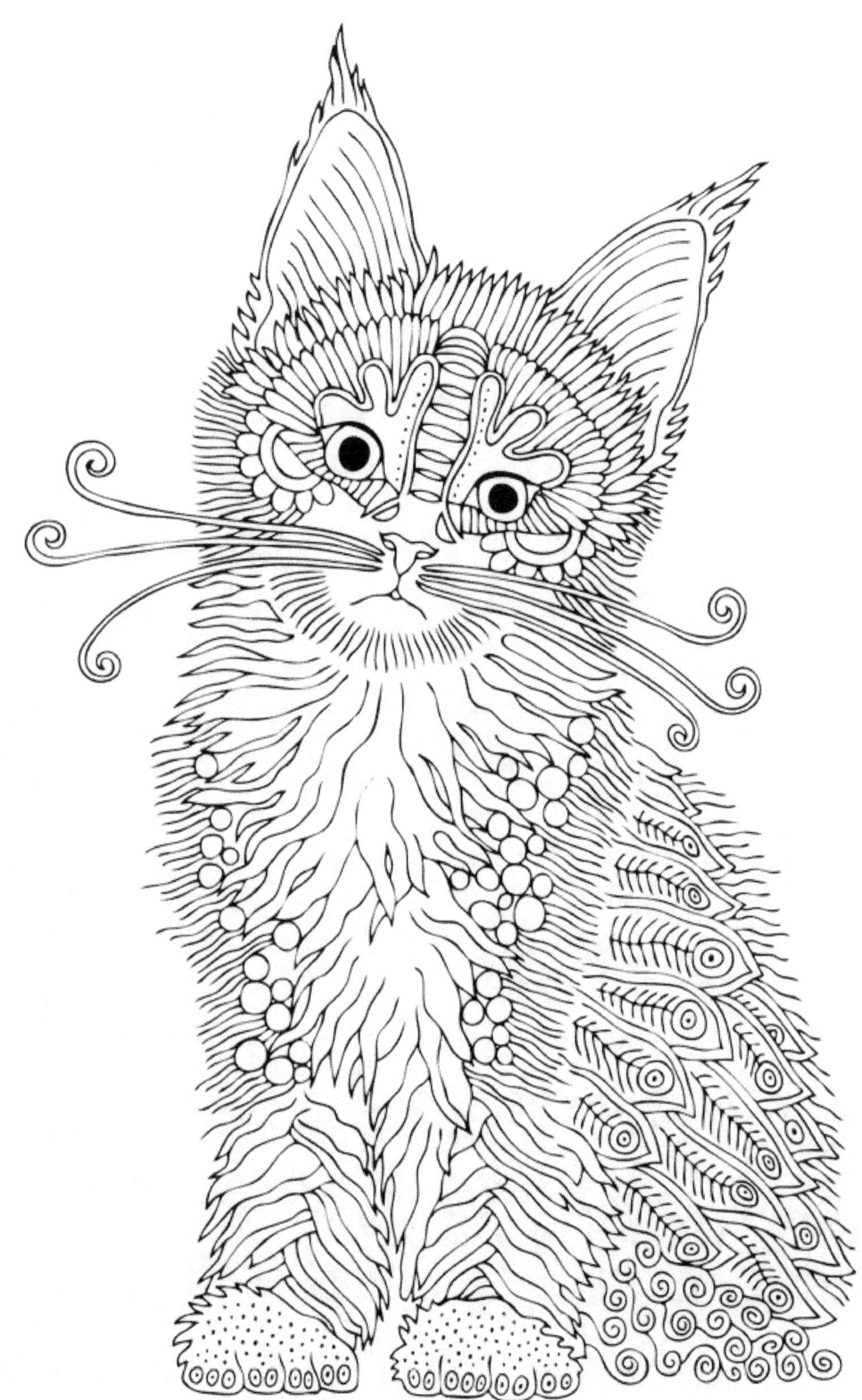

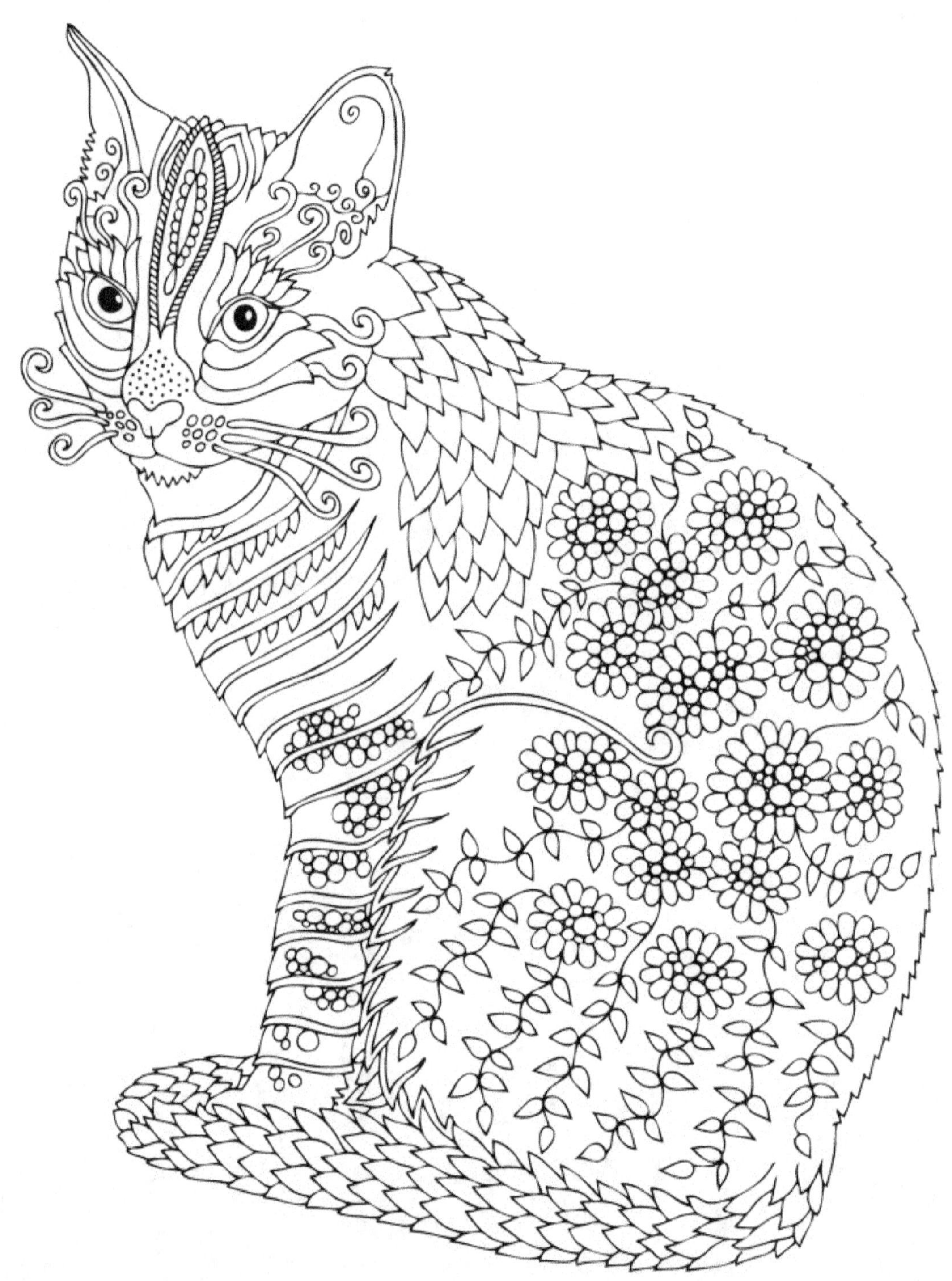

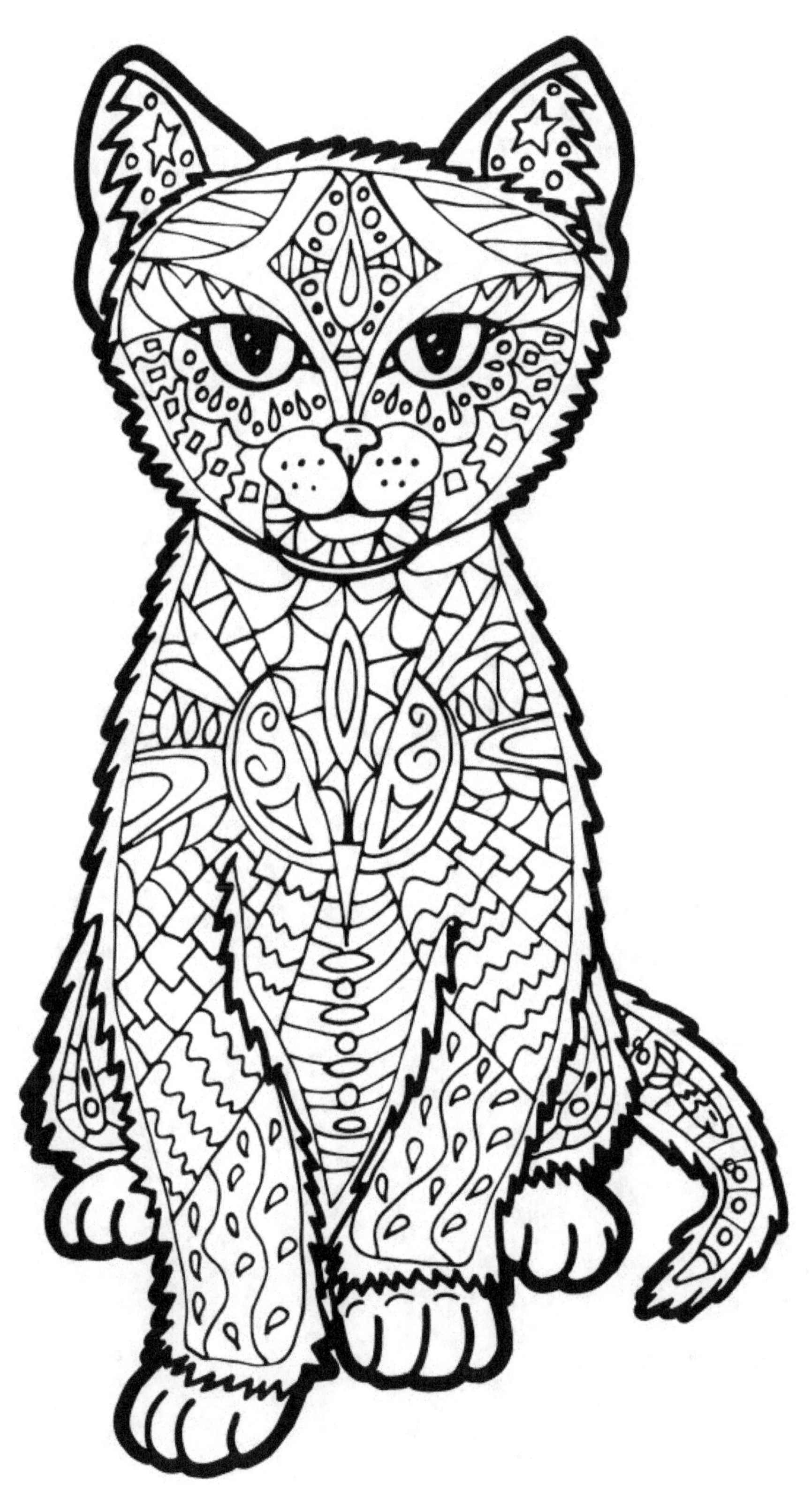

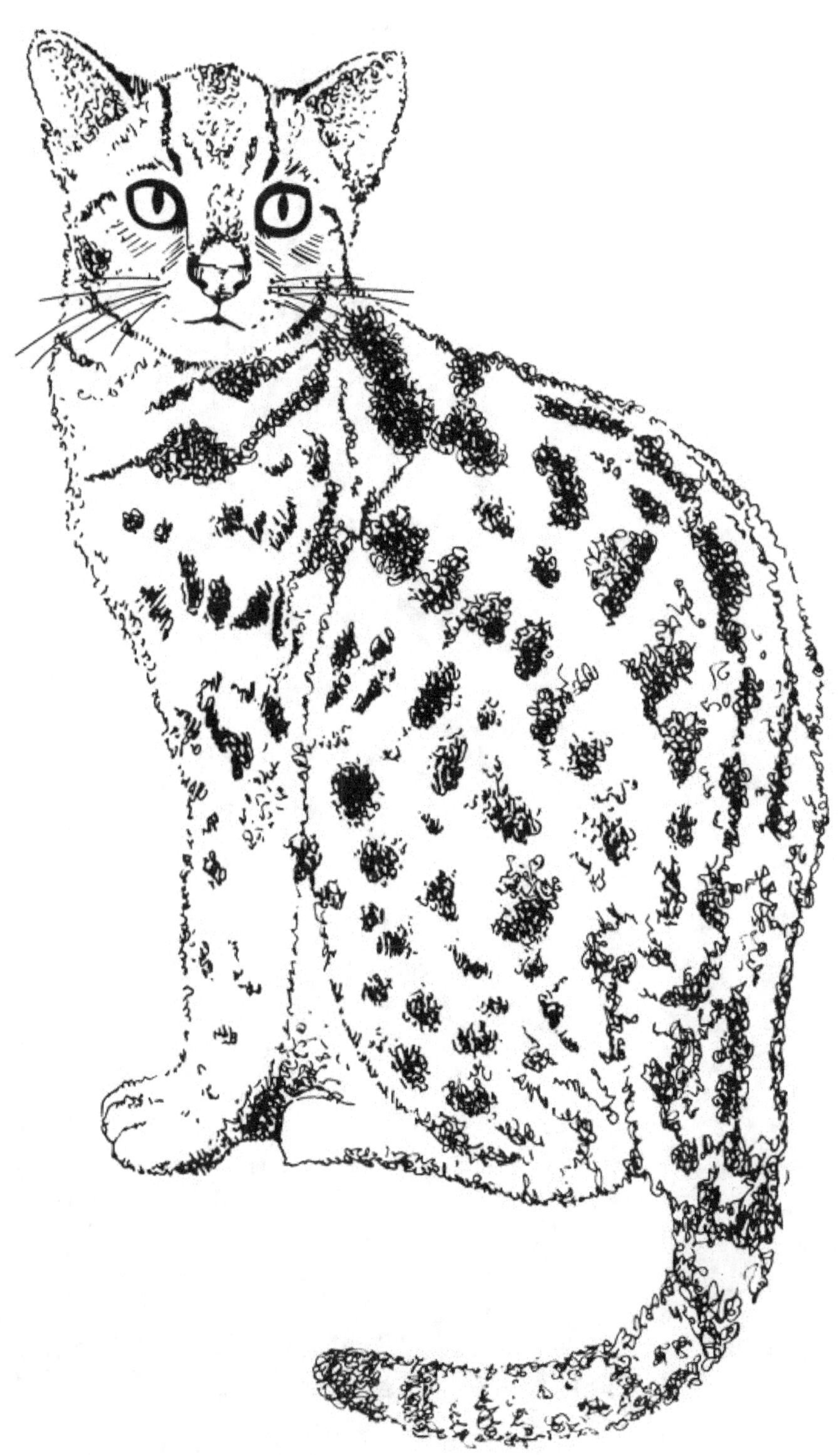

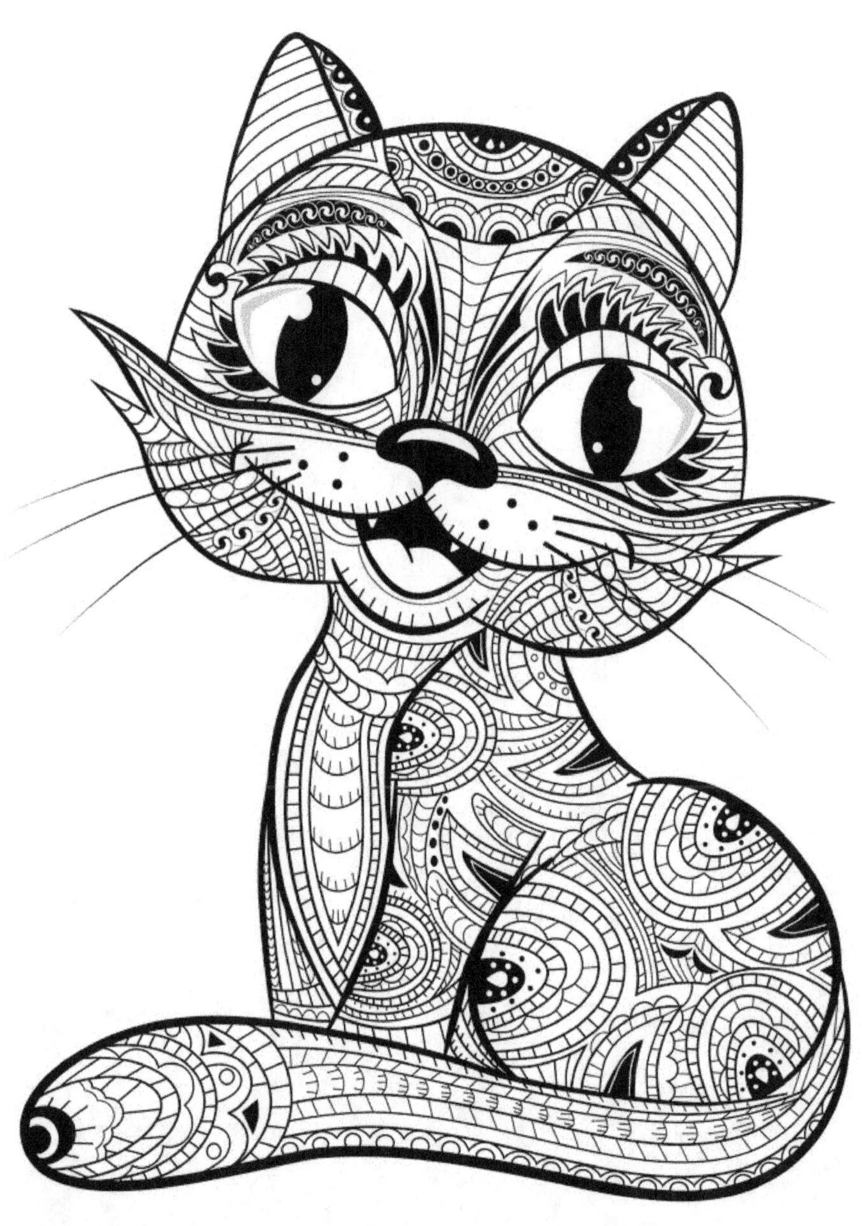

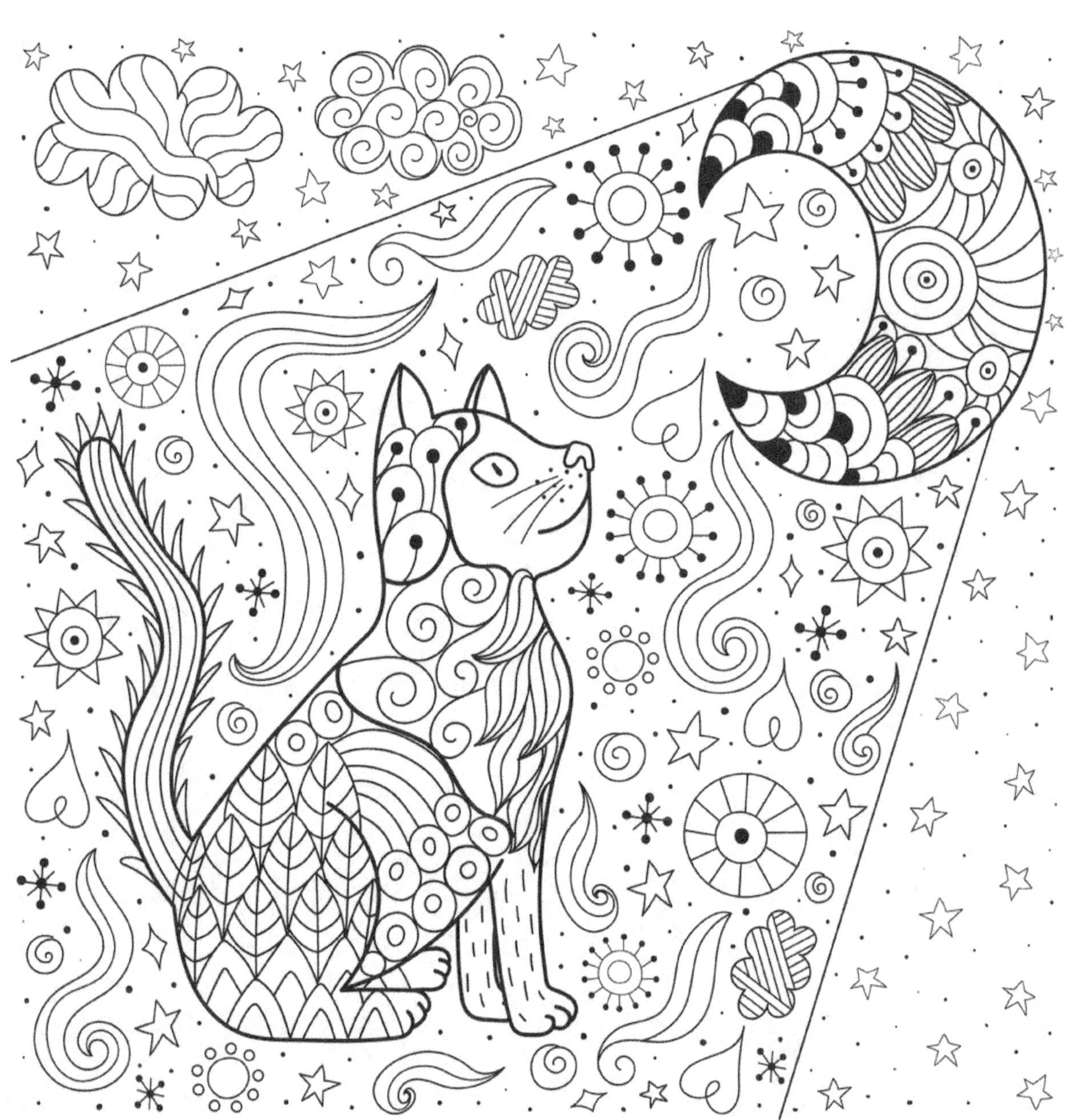

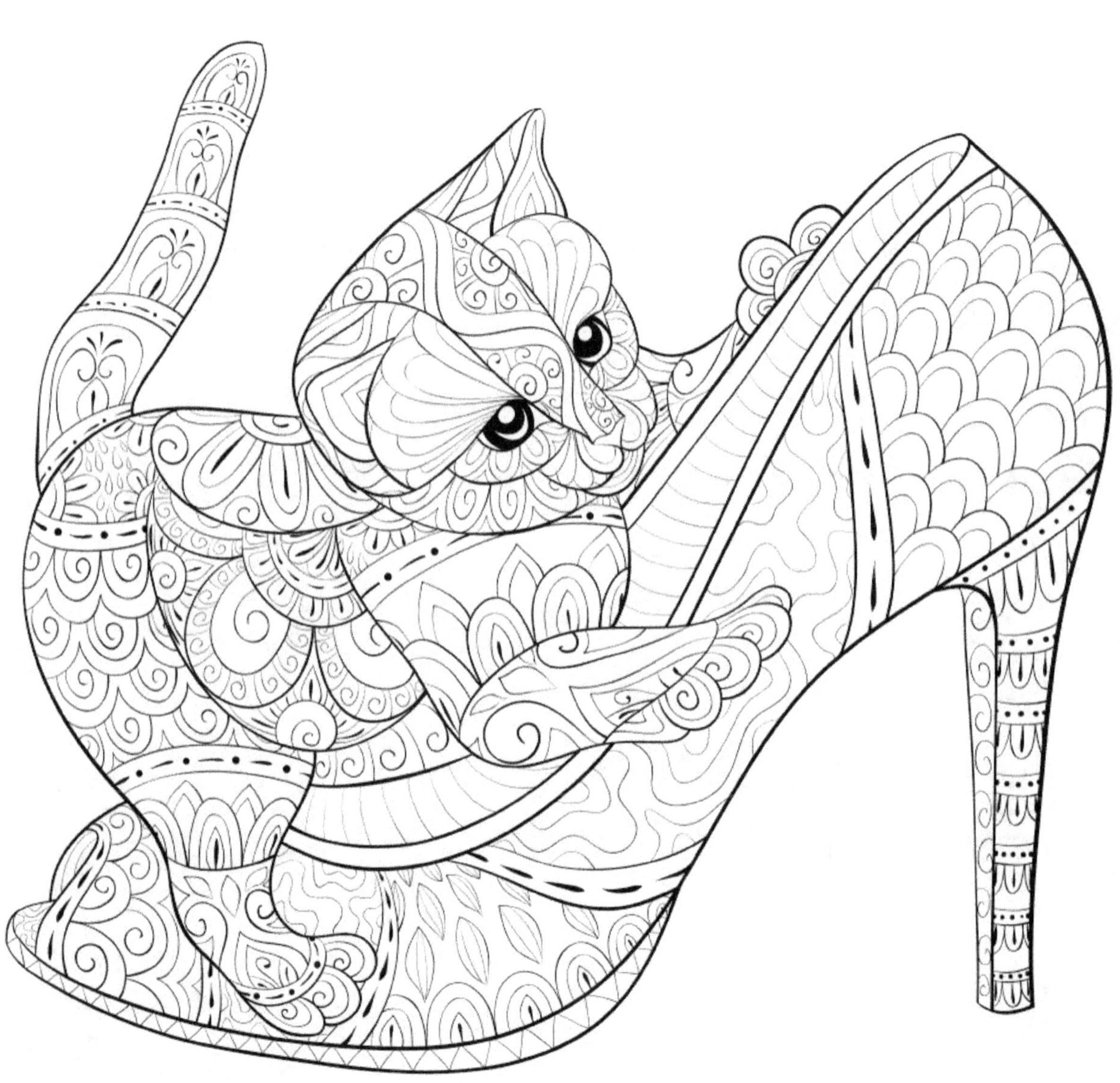

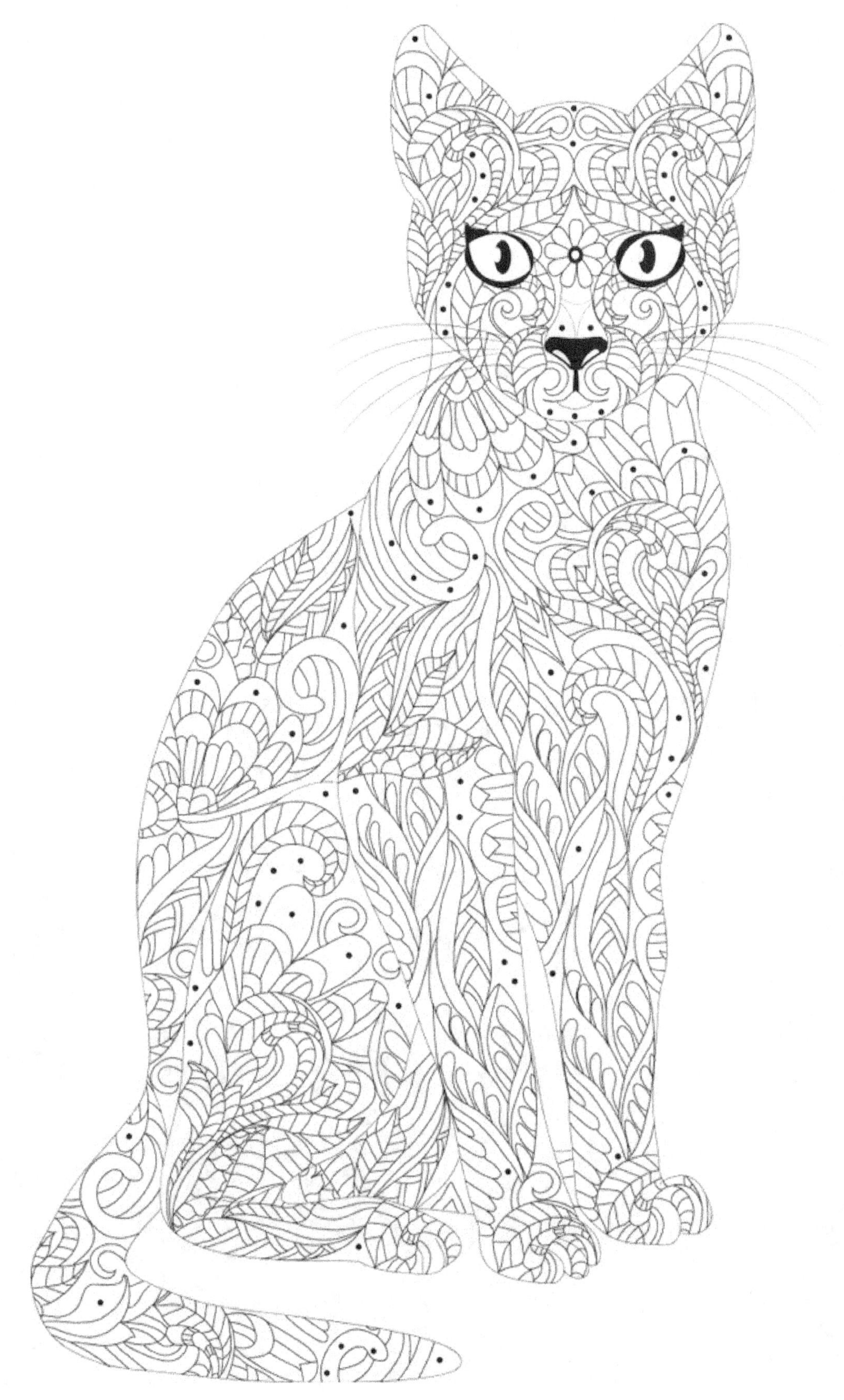

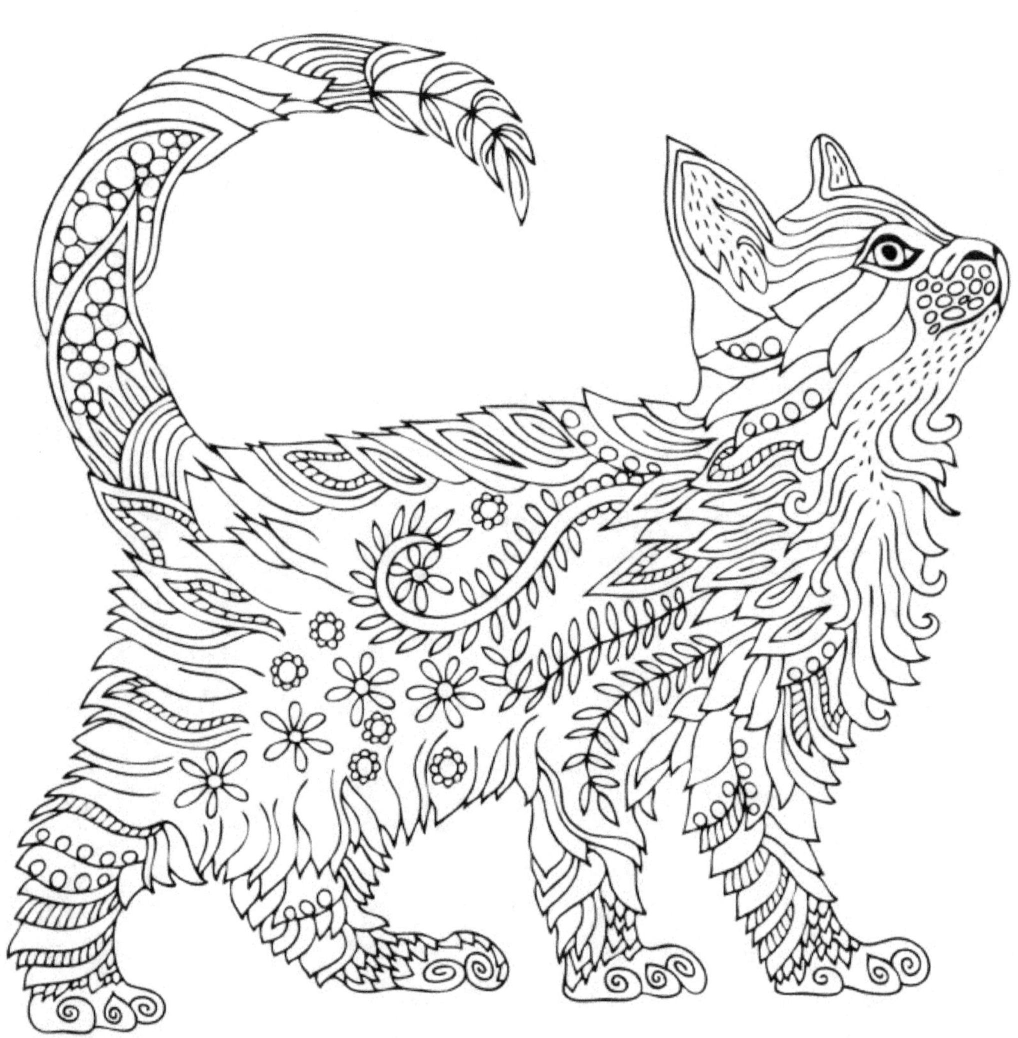

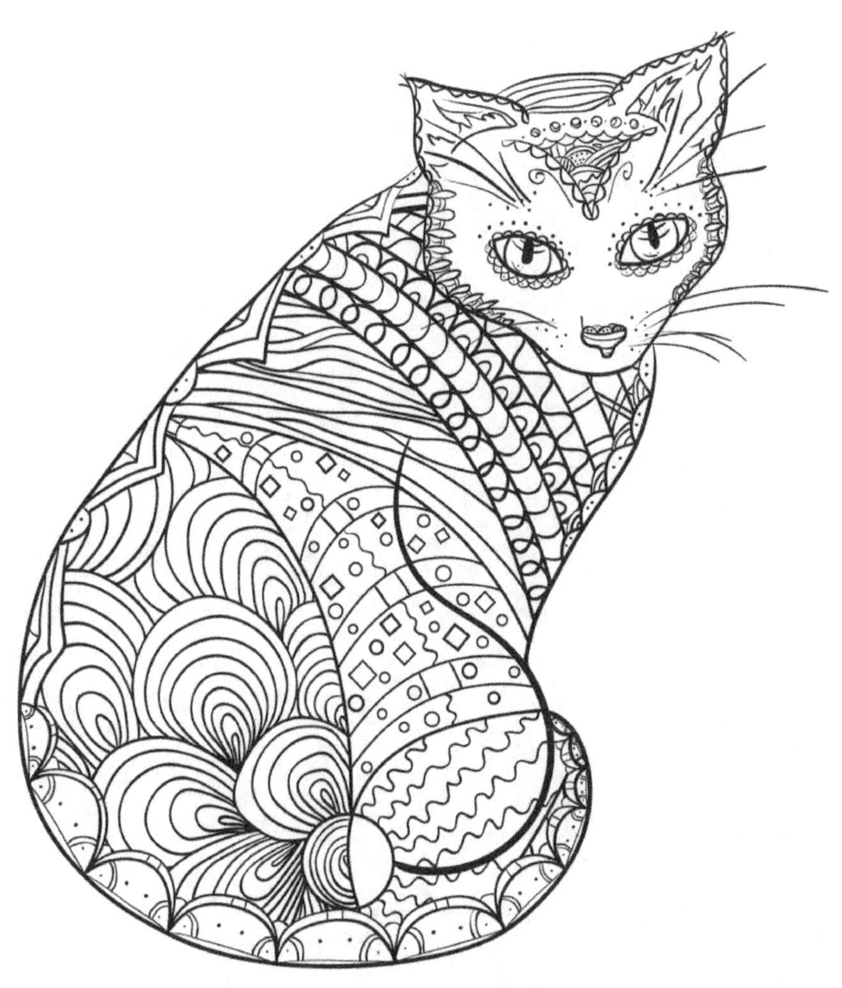

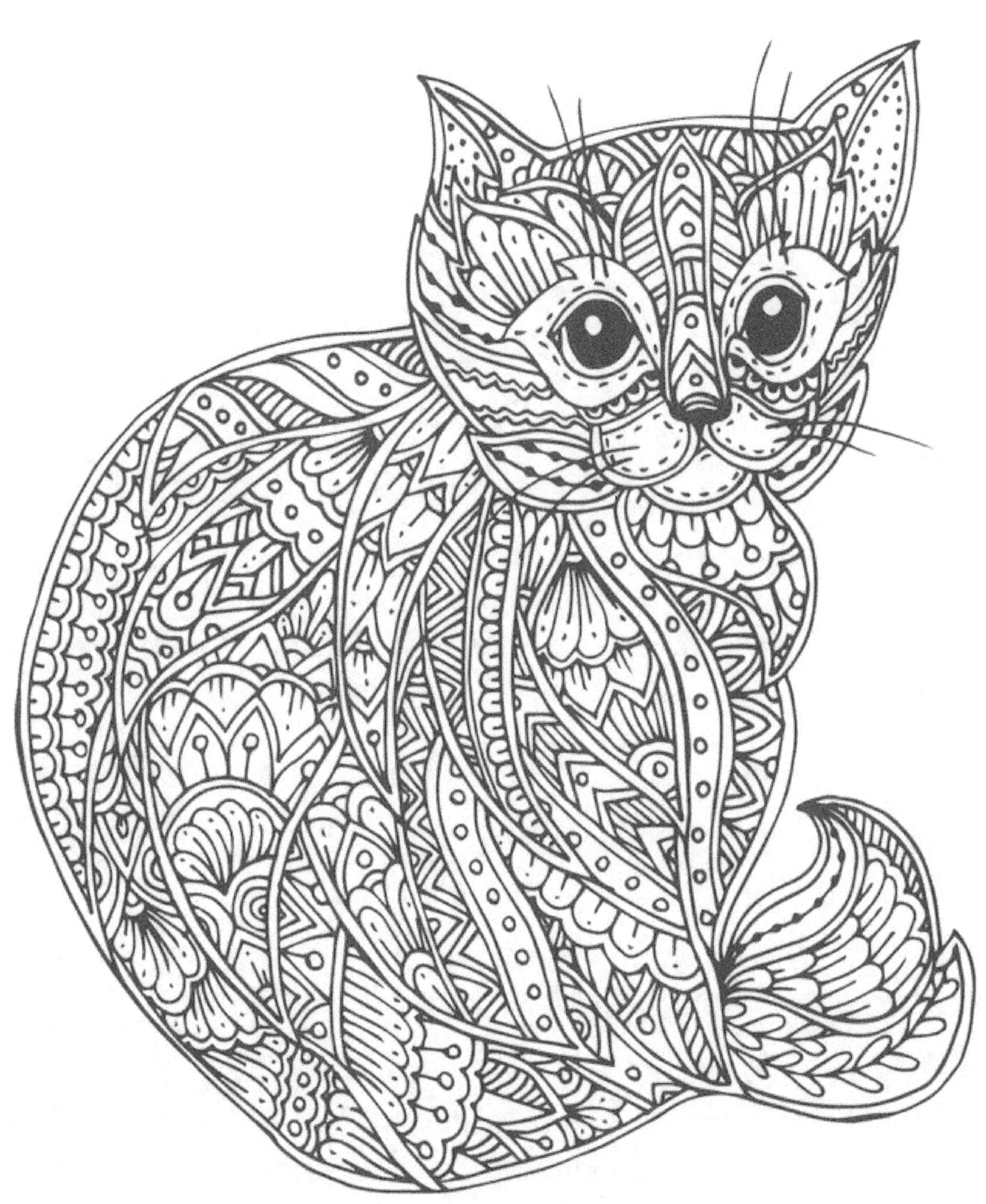

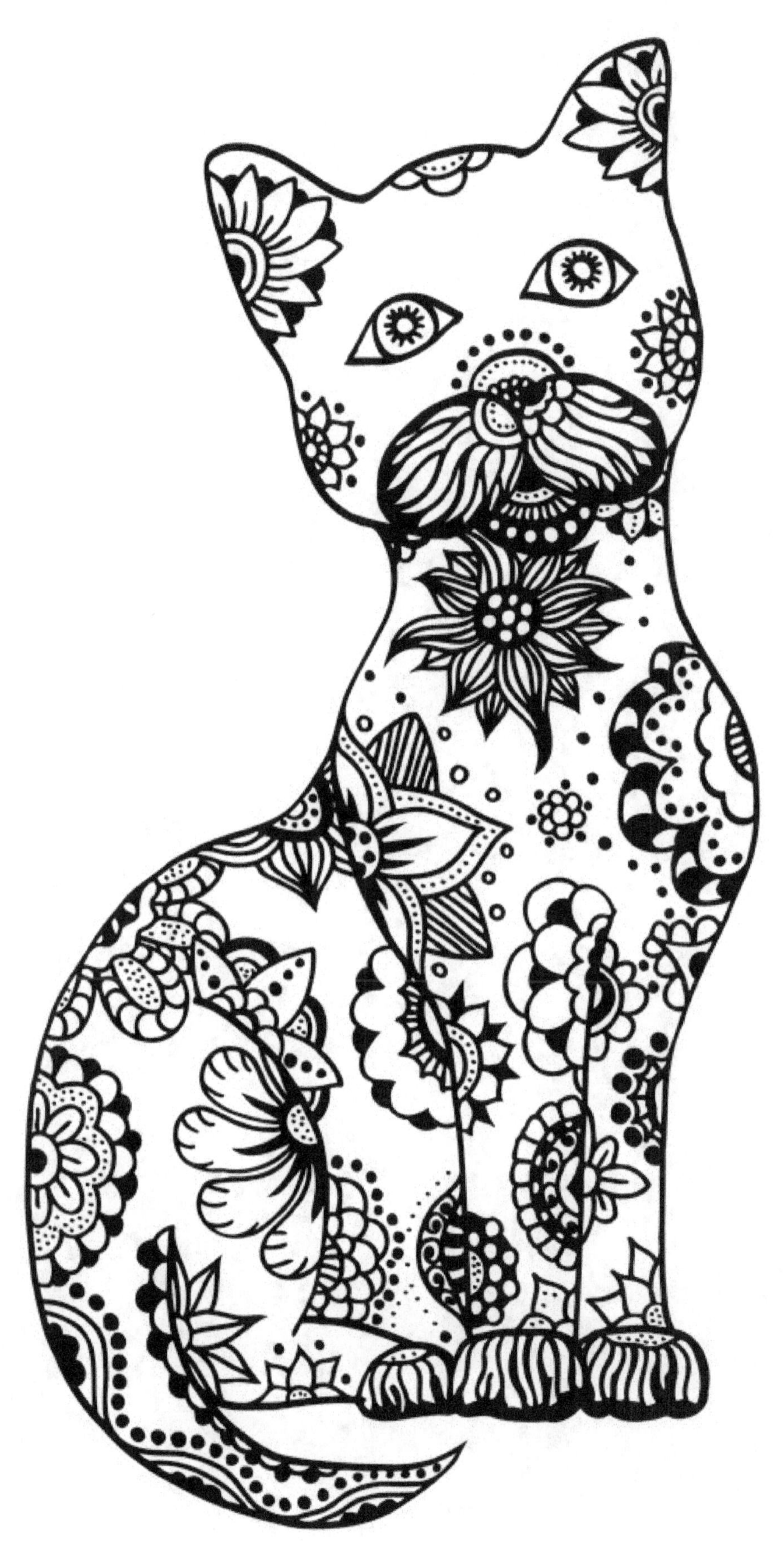